Is Affirmative Action Fair?

Debating Race

ion Fair?

The Myth of Equity in College Admissions

NATASHA WARIKOO

polity

First published in 2023 by Polity Press

Polity Press
65 Bridge Street
Cambridge CB2 1UR, UK

Polity Press
111 River Street
Hoboken, NJ 07030, USA

ISBN-13: 978-1-5095-4936-8
ISBN-13: 978-1-5095-4937-5(pb)

A catalogue record for this book is available from the British Library.

Library of Congress Control Number: 2022937423

Typeset in 11 on 15pt Adobe Garamond Pro
by Fakenham Prepress Solutions, Fakenham, Norfolk NR21 8NL
Printed and bound in Great Britain by CPI Group (UK) Ltd, Croydon

For further information on Polity, visit our website:
politybooks.com

CONTENTS

For decades, considering whether an applicant is part of an underrepresented racial group when making selection decisions has been a topic of much public debate. When they hear the words *affirmative action*, most Americans have a visceral response. Some think it's essential. Others think it is a violation of their rights. Most will have a view, and a strong one at that. And nearly always, our very strong opinions hinge on a very simple question—whether we think affirmative action is *fair* or not. When we talk about affirmative action, we are nearly always asking questions about core American values: whether we truly are a meritocracy, if we can (or should) legislate against racial injustice, how to best harness the power of education. Like abortion, this issue seems to polarize us even though our views are more similar than we believe they are. My aim is that by the end of this book, whatever your beliefs, you will have a deeper understanding of affirmative action and its value for higher education and for American society, more broadly.

Affirmative action arose in the United States during the 1960s as the federal government and universities attempted to increase opportunities for and representation of African Americans in government contracts, selective colleges, and beyond.[1] It was one practice of the growing civil rights agenda. While affirmative action today is indelibly linked to liberals—and almost universally despised by conservatives—this was not always the case. Democratic President Bill Clinton didn't think that affirmative action should be ended, although he did argue that we should "mend it" (but "not end it"); several decades earlier, Republican President Richard Nixon actually *expanded* affirmative action in federal employment.[2]

Though affirmative action is a painfully divisive topic, our views on the practice are actually quite complex, and seem to depend on the question we are asked and how the issue is framed. Six in ten Americans respond favorably when asked "Do you generally favor or oppose affirmative action programs for racial minorities?"[3] And when college students are asked to choose from two candidates with similar backgrounds in a simulated admissions decision, even students who say they "oppose affirmative action" tend to pick the one from an underrepresented group.[4] But when posed using the possibility of "reverse discrimination," support drops: in a 2021 survey, Americans were asked:

> *Some people say that because of past discrimination, Blacks should be given preference in hiring and promotion. Others say that such preference in hiring and promotion of Blacks is wrong because it discriminates against whites. What about your opinion—are you for or against preferential hiring and promotion of Blacks?*

Just 23 percent expressed support.[5]

While affirmative action plays a role in private sector hiring and government contracts, we seem to hear the loudest debates when it comes to college admissions. When selective colleges decide whether to admit an applicant, affirmative action means they take into consideration whether an applicant is part of a racial group that is underrepresented on campus. Over 300 of our selective colleges do so.[6] In addition to considering race, most also consider an applicant's SAT or ACT scores, grade point average (GPA), number of advanced-level courses, personal essays, teacher recommendations, and extracurricular activities. Some also consider an interview, requests from athletic coaches ("athletic recruiting"), ties to the university ("legacy" status), and whether a student needs financial assistance. The most elite colleges are even more specific—they look to have representation from all fifty states, students with a range of intended majors, diversity of parent professions, and much more.[7] These criteria are considered together as part of a "holistic" process—the US Supreme court has prohibited specific points or quotas for racial groups. Applicants from underrepresented groups on selective college campuses—African Americans, Native Americans, and Latinx—are given the benefit of the doubt if, for example, their test scores are marginally lower than similar white applicants.[8]

The increasing demand—within and beyond the United States—for a limited number of seats at the most selective universities means that the question of fairness in admissions weighs heavily on the minds of many. The more parents believe that where their children go to college matters as the first step toward securing their futures, and as a marker of identity as someone "smart" and "worthy" of elite education, the stronger their opinions seem to be on what a fair system of selection entails. Rapidly declining admit rates to top colleges—for instance, Harvard University's admit rate for undergraduates is now less than 4 percent, down from 6 percent just ten years ago and 12 percent in 1997—fuels this sense of insecurity about the future.[9]

It is not just parents who care. Elite colleges have a sacred quality, even to many of us who have never set foot on their campuses. They symbolize the American dream—something achievable by anyone with some talent and a strong work ethic. And we Americans like it this way—in the United States we believe, more than our European counterparts, in the importance of meritocracy: that one's standard of living should follow from one's effort and skills, and that addressing inequality means focusing on providing equal opportunities to everyone rather than supporting everyone in society regardless of their level of accomplishment.[10] The very American individualism that French thinker Alexis de Tocqueville identified nearly two hundred years ago seems stronger than ever today.[11] Our persistent individualism means we assume, and even insist, that admissions should be tied to individual achievements.

Political actors, too, have played a role in ensuring loud public debate on affirmative action. Conservative activists have strategically attacked it, employing the language of civil rights and racial justice in their critiques.[12] They argue that affirmative action amounts to racial discrimination toward whites (and sometimes, toward Asian Americans, who are mostly not eligible for affirmative action in college admissions).[13] Aside from organizing and funding multiple lawsuits since the 1970s that have landed in the US Supreme Court, conservative activists have also launched anti–affirmative action ballot initiatives in seven states to date, six of which have been successful. In addition, they have successfully pushed three more state bans by executive order or new state laws.[14] To the question of "Is affirmative action fair?" these actors have voiced a resounding "No!" On the other hand, liberal defenders of affirmative action have loudly defended the policy as a cornerstone of an elite college education.[15] Advocates attempted to repeal California's 1998 ban through a 2020 referendum (but narrowly lost that vote).

Central to the framing of public debates over affirmative action is the notion of fairness. Is it fair to consider race, given our commitments to judging each person on their individual merits and not discriminating on the basis of race? Is it fair *not* to consider race, given the historical exclusion of certain racial minorities from elite college campuses, and from the American dream? What is a fair system of selection, anyway? The answers to these questions rest, in part, on our understanding of fairness in society. Some see treating everyone as a blank slate as the fairest mechanism, while others think fairness means considering a person's accomplishments in light of the opportunities and roadblocks they have experienced. Some see the lack of significant numbers of Black, Latinx, and Native American students on campus as a sign of admissions gone awry, while others do not. And, in any case, all these perspectives, as we'll see, fail to consider what colleges are trying to *do* when they admit students.

These questions of individual merit can all seem rather abstract and hypothetical; the real reason why affirmative action is so divisive is because it forces us to address America's most divisive issue: race. Our views on affirmative action depend in large part on how we make sense of differences in achievement by race. If you oppose affirmative action, chances are you believe that racial gaps in achievement are related to cultural differences in commitments to academic excellence and willingness to work hard; you might also feel threatened by policies designed to address racial inequality.[16] Your views are likely best described as "colorblind," because in your view the only fair way to address race is to ignore it, even if you feel that racial inequality is a problem.[17] Otherwise, we are strengthening a social category that has been used historically to disenfranchise vulnerable groups, and implying that those groups are inherently inferior. In the words of US Supreme Court Chief Justice John Roberts, "The way to stop discrimination on the basis of race is to stop discriminating on the basis of race."[18] But while you may view your attitudes as philosophical, studies of racial attitudes have shown, in fact, that opposition to policies like affirmative action are correlated with racial prejudice, even when we compare people with the same political views.[19] Legal attacks on affirmative action rely on non-discrimination laws—designed to protect stigmatized minorities—to make the argument that affirmative action is actually racist toward whites (and, sometimes, toward Asian Americans). Many of these opponents also argue that it sets its supposed beneficiaries up for failure when they enter colleges in which they are not academically prepared to be successful.[20]

If you support affirmative action, chances are you see the world rather differently. You probably believe that race differences are fundamentally rooted in this country's social policies, and that centuries of racial discrimination and exclusion continue to create disadvantage for Black, Native American, and Latinx youth. The history of race in the United States has shaped everything from dramatic wealth differences between white and Black Americans, to which neighborhoods Americans live in, to whether a birthright citizen is perceived as truly American or even personally warm.[21] Given the history of race in the United States, proponents of affirmative action point out that race—due to both historical circumstances as well as present perceptions and economic resources— continues to affect the life chances, lived experiences, material realities, and perspectives of Americans. Most who recognize the ongoing social meaning of race in American society agree that ignoring race alone will not make those realities vanish. Any hope for racial equality requires actively addressing race; thus, affirmative action is important for fostering a more just, democratic society.

In addition to the reality of racial inequality, if you're a proponent of affirmative action you might also recognize that people from different racial backgrounds are likely to hold different perspectives on the world, and that diversity is valuable for classroom and late-night discussions. Similarly, you might feel that an all-white government would feel a little less legitimate, or at least, a little less adequate to govern us all. To ensure a quorum of qualified minority leaders, this argument goes, we need affirmative action to counter other barriers that society, directly or indirectly, imposes on underrepresented groups. Under this view, affirmative action makes important contributions to a campus and to American society as a whole, not just to the individual who is admitted because of it.

So what is right? Should selective colleges continue to consider race in admissions? The answer to this question is a lot more complex than you may think.

In this book I am going to ask you to question the terms of this debate. Political philosophers have argued that selection for any social good—spots at an elite college, coveted jobs, or anything else in high demand—should be based on how to achieve the most just outcomes. No one *deserves* to be selected. This means that "merit" is inherently situational—it depends on what would benefit a particular society in a particular moment in time, and those needs are not static.[22] The same could be said about organizations: they should evaluate people and select from them based on what the organization needs in a particular moment. In other words, no one is *entitled* to be admitted to a selective college, no matter their accomplishments.[23] Indeed, how colleges view the best, most fair way to select students has dramatically changed over time.[24] Even today, countries diverge in how they allocate university seats to prospective students when there are more interested students than spots available. To see affirmative action policies as a threat to fairness is to take a short-sighted view of what justice in college admissions might mean.

As simple as it may seem, without a shared under-standing of the purposes of elite higher education we are hard pressed to determine whether affirmative action within admissions is the right thing to do. This analysis requires a deep dive into the purposes of higher education, to understand the role of admissions in the organizational purposes of our selective colleges and universities. In Chapter 1 of this book I do just that. These are complex organizations with multiple stakeholders and multiple organizational goals that have shifted over time. We like to think of universities as ideal temples of learning, equity, and meritocracy but in reality they are complex organizations with many needs. The admissions process is one way that, for better and worse, the university meets those needs; once we accept that, admission no longer is the certification of an individual's worthiness or deservingness. After establishing this framework, I turn to the practice of affirmative action in the context of the purposes of higher education.

In Chapter 2 I assess arguments for and against affirmative action in college admissions. As you'll see, I am a social scientist who relies on evidence to assess the common arguments made to defend or critique affirmative action. Analyzing data allows me to step away from the heated debates and instead analytically consider claims. I consider four arguments in favor of affirmative action: it facilitates the learning of all students by bringing diverse perspectives to the college classroom; it makes important contributions to society; it promotes equal opportunity; and it serves as a mechanism for reparations for past wrongs toward specific minority groups. I also consider two common critiques: affirmative action is a form of racial discrimination toward whites and Asian Americans, and those who get admitted through it will not be able to succeed in the colleges to which they are admitted because they are underprepared.

In Chapter 3 I take Asian Americans as a case study to make sense of the arguments for and against affirmative action. Today's racial landscape is far more complex than a Black-white binary, even though our discussions about race too often get stuck on that dividing line. On the one hand, Asian Americans are academically outperforming all race groups, including whites, and are sometimes used to suggest that racial inequality does not affect educational opportunities, so there should be no affirmative action.[25] On the other hand, racist attacks on Asian Americans are on the rise, and some Asian American groups have very low levels of income and education. With the Asian American population in the United States rapidly increasing—Asian Americans are the fastest-growing racial group in the United States today—these issues have grown in salience.[26] In fact, in the latest anti-affirmative action lawsuit to be heard by the United States Supreme Court a group of Asian American plaintiffs is suing Harvard University for racial discrimination in admissions, for which their proposed remedy is an end to all race-based considerations in admissions.

I'll conclude this book by arguing that "fairness" is the wrong question to be asking. It centers the question of whether whites (and sometimes, Asian Americans) suffer harm when race is taken into consideration in admissions. Instead, we should ask whether affirmative action furthers the mission of selective colleges. I realize this is an unusual perspective and it may not shift your thinking. But I am going to try to convince you to reframe how you think about college admissions, and in turn, how you think about affirmative action.

My empirical analyses make clear that affirmative action enables colleges to build a better society: by increasing educational opportunities, furthering racial justice, providing a better educational experience to all students, identifying hidden talent, and diversifying our leadership. Still, given the complexity of the purposes of higher education, there is no single "best" way to select students, and claims about selecting the very "best" applicants are problematic and drive many misconceptions about college admissions. Taking this view will help us all to take our attention off the flashpoint controversies and anxieties about race, and instead to find new solutions for selective college admissions going forward.

CHAPTER 1

The Purposes of Higher Education and the History of Affirmative Action

What is lost in the feverish debate over affirmative action is the bigger question beneath it: how should a college decide who to accept? Should a college prioritize teaching the most academically accomplished students? Or the ones who have had limited opportunities but show the most potential to learn quickly? Or the ones who are the furthest *behind*? Given the disciplinary nature of universities, should selection ensure a quorum of students intending to study each subject (thus prioritizing students interested in studying philosophy since they are much less common than those interested in studying business); or should universities instead respond to student demand by adjusting the sizes of their departments?[1] And beyond these academic considerations, there are countless others. Should colleges admit those with top athletic skills (even if those skills are virtually unattainable by students from working-class families with little access to private sports coaching and recruitment camps), or should they ignore non-academic accomplishments altogether?[2] Should they prioritize those who have shown leadership potential? Those whose families contribute to the financial livelihood of the university, or those growing up in poverty? Should the likelihood of bettering our society be considered? Can we as a society agree on these qualities, and even if we can, can we agree on measures of them? These potential criteria are as numerous as they are complex; no single college, let alone the entire country, has been able to offer a clear and sustained answer to what an admissions office should prioritize. Considering these near-impossible questions, however, leads to two broader questions at the heart of college admissions. First, what is the purpose of elite higher education, and how should institutions select students to further that purpose? Second, how can they select students to achieve those goals in the best manner? The answers to these questions are remarkably unclear.

In a series of lectures in 1963 that became a seminal book, Clark Kerr, the president of the University of California system, highlighted how US universities had become "multiversities"—that is, organizations beholden to multiple purposes and goals: teaching, research, and the public good. Kerr noted this shift from past models: British universities historically focused on teaching, German universities on research, and American land-grant universities on the public good through practical knowledge. [3] By the 1960s, US universities were trying to do all three, within a polyglot community of humanists, social scientists, scientists, nonacademic personnel, administrators, and students.[4] A recent study of college mission statements found that these three goals endure: most express commitments to teaching as well as the public good, including inculcating civic values in students; doctorate-granting universities also express commitments to research.[5]

In addition to the three purposes outlined by Kerr, today commitments to diversity are commonly expressed in college mission statements, and we also look to higher education to address social inequality. [6] In previous generations a college degree was considered an elite degree meant for a small minority of high school graduates. But by 2015 President Obama called for universal higher education, because of its promise for improving the life chances of economically disadvantaged Americans.[7] Colleges promote this vision, too. Colleges large and small, selective and not, consistently emphasize to prospective students the lifelong benefits of a degree from their institutions.[8] Now that a college degree seems more important than ever, these questions are of critical importance.

How can (and should) an admissions office attend to these goals of research, teaching, social mobility, and the public good? Research is the least relevant to admissions, since it is the purview of the faculty, not students; but faculty may have an interest in admitting students most likely to go on to become researchers like themselves. In terms of teaching, universities need to decide whether to focus on teaching top students at the highest level possible, or weaker students who may grow the most from being taught; selective colleges have generally gone for the former, striving to improve their status by admitting stronger and stronger students as measured by, for example, the average SAT score of admitted students.[9]

Further, when we consider the goal of social mobility, it remains even more unclear why previous academic achievement is such a central focus. We could argue that college should actually play the *opposite* role to what it currently plays. If college education is to promote social mobility, perhaps admission should be akin to means-tested social supports—provided to those who need it most, whether because of the financial hardships their parents experienced, racial exclusion, or weak academic skills. Former Harvard Law School professor Lani Guinier famously argued that we should consider college admissions as a mechanism to facilitate a more robust democracy and when we do so, it should lead us to discard standardized testing as a part of the application process, in favor of broad inclusiveness and representation.[10]

The fourth goal, contributing to the public good, is capacious enough to encompass myriad criteria for admission, but perhaps so capacious that the implications for selection are exceedingly unclear. Should universities scrutinize admissions essays for evidence that an applicant envisions a future in public service? Holds an entrepreneurial spirit or leadership capacity? And do we have any evidence on how to measure the likelihood of someone actually following through on these aspirations, especially for those who have not had opportunities to demonstrate their potential?

In short, our common conceptions of the admissions process only obliquely align with the primary goals of a university, which is odd when you think about it, and further evidence of how complicated and obtuse admissions ultimately is. Beyond these four very amorphous goals, there are other expectations for an admissions office related to less grand university goals. Many colleges look to place top athletes on university sports teams (who, in turn, bolster school spirit, publicity, and sometimes dollars from ticket and team merchandise sales); to bring a quorum of children of alumni to campus to ensure loyalty and financial support; and to award only a limited amount of financial aid dollars so that student tuition ensures the university can pay for all its programs, buildings, and amenities.[11] Like all organizations, universities also need to ensure their future existence, and admissions plays an important role in that goal, as well.

The job of the admissions office, then, is not to find some uniform definition of the "best" student, but rather to select students that further the myriad university goals and organizational needs. In other words, while students, parents, and guidance counselors often view college admissions as a contest of achievement and deservingness, the reality is much more complex. Those seeking seats in elite colleges see their individual achievements as the path to a seat, but a university admissions office may not view its role as an award selection committee. Admission to a selective college, unlike awards, is about university goals, rather than certification of individual worthiness, as many believe.

And this is how it should be. There is no inherently best way to define and measure whether a given student is worthy of a spot at a given school—rather, "merit" is socially defined. It depends on the prevailing norms in a society or organization (Do we value skills in science? The humanities? Writing skills? Math skills?

Leadership skills?). It also depends on what an organization needs (Does the baseball team need a pitcher? Does the university need donors who may give more if their children gain a leg up in admissions?). Given the whims of what a particular college is looking for in any given year, philosopher Michael Sandel once imagined a letter admissions offices might send to admitted students:

> *We are pleased to inform you that your application for admission has been accepted. Through no doing of your own, it turns out that you happen to have the traits that society needs at the moment. . . . No praise is intended or to be inferred from this decision, as your having the relevant qualities is arbitrary from a moral point of view. You are to be congratulated, not in the sense that you deserve credit for having the qualities that led to your admission—you do not—but only in the sense that the winner of a lottery is to be congratulated. You are lucky to have come along with the right traits at the right moment, and if you choose to accept our offer you will ultimately be entitled to the benefits that attach to being used in this way. . . . You, or more likely your parents, may be tempted to celebrate in the further sense that you take this admission to reflect favorably, if not on your native endowments, at least on the conscientious effort you have made to cultivate your abilities and overcome the obstacles*

to your achievements. But the assumption that you deserve
even the superior character necessary to your effort is
equally problematic, for your character also depends on
fortunate circumstances of various kinds for which you
can claim no credit. . . . We look forward nonetheless to
seeing you in the fall.[12]

Sandel's letter, though farcical, highlights the contradiction between admissions in practice and admissions in the eyes of most applicants, their families, and the broader society.

It is hard to discard the idea that colleges simply choose the "best" students. The reality—that colleges are organizations trying to fulfill their needs, year after year—is more complex. Unlike the labor market, for which we understand that an applicant is chosen for a job based on what a company needs, not because they are the "best" applicant, in higher education so often we describe admission as a reward for hard work and dedication. It is the very backbone of our very American beliefs in equal opportunity. But seeing admissions as a competition to decide who is the most deserving reinforces this misguided faith—that college admissions, like American life in general, is an individualist meritocracy, and an equitable one at that. Even though we may know better, this individualist meritocracy idea remains central to how applicants and their families view admissions today: a contest that rewards the very "best," "most deserving" applicants to a college.

Who can blame the families and high school educators intent on viewing selective college admissions as an individual contest of meritocracy, in which there is an assumed shared understanding of merit? American culture abounds with references to "smart" young people attending elite colleges. Movies like *The Social Network* dramatize the smarts of students attending elite colleges. *The Chair,* starring Sandra Oh, chronicles life on an elite college campus with its academically stellar students. Particularly in upper-middle-class families, one's alma mater and where one's children go on to college are important markers of identity and perceived worthiness. Parents and kids often put a sticker of their alma mater or their child's college on the backs of their cars, signaling identity and status; we rarely see stickers of nonselective colleges on cars. Every year newspapers pick up on stories about students admitted to every single Ivy League college, declining admit rates at top colleges, and more. [13] We don't see nearly as many (if any) articles, in contrast, about other systems of selection—how many jobs graduating seniors were offered, for example, or how many applicants per position were received by employers.

So while universities may strive to further multiple goals that may require different criteria (including affirmative action), many of which are tied to collective goals for society, applicants generally seek individual advancement. What does this bode for affirmative action? I turn next to the history of considering race in college admissions. Whether we support affirmative action depends in part on which function of the multiversity we emphasize, and what it is we expect universities to do.

Affirmative Action

The federal government started using the term *affirmative action* in the 1960s. President Kennedy first used the term in an executive order barring discrimination in hiring or treatment by any company receiving a federal contract. In 1965, that passive requirement— not discriminating—became an active requirement, when President Lyndon Johnson signed an executive order requiring firms that received federal contracts to take specific, documented actions to increase diversity in their firms. Johnson famously said,

You do not take a person who, for years, has been hobbled by chains and liberate him, bring him up to the starting line of a race and then say, "You are free to compete with all the others," and still justly believe that you have been completely fair. Thus it is not enough just to open the gates of opportunity. All our citizens must have the ability to walk through those gates.[14]

Just as the government sought to ensure that federal contractors gave a fair shot to minority jobseekers, selective private colleges were considering how to address the near absence of African American students on their campuses. By the time the Civil Rights Act of 1964 was passed, multiple private and public universities were already considering race in admissions to admit greater numbers of African American students—their way of addressing racial inequity.[15] The numbers of Black students admitted under those programs were miniscule—often less than twenty per year on a given campus—but they grew rapidly over the subsequent decade. Eventually, Native American and Latinx applicants were also considered under affirmative action.

As affirmative action grew, some pushed back and claimed it amounted to "reverse discrimination" toward whites—that is, that racial discrimination in the United States was now enacted not just toward

African Americans, but also toward whites in the form of affirmative action. This pushback soon resulted in legal challenges, which centered on the US Constitution's Fourteenth Amendment, passed after the end of slavery to protect African Americans. The amendment's Equal Protection Clause requires "strict scrutiny" when an organization makes distinctions using a characteristic deemed "suspect" by the US Supreme Court, such as race or religion. Differentiation based on those suspect categories is allowed only if it is "narrowly tailored" (that is, uses the suspect category as little as possible) and doing so advances a "compelling state interest." The Fourteenth Amendment was invoked in the landmark *Brown v. Board of Education* case that outlawed racially segregated schools. In the case of affirmative action, however, the Fourteenth Amendment has been used to try to secure privileges for whites (and in the case of recent lawsuits, Asian Americans) over Black, Native American, and Latinx applicants.[16]

In a landmark 1978 decision, *Regents of the University of California v. Bakke*, the US Supreme Court ruled that the University of California, Davis medical school could not reserve a specific number of spots for underrepresented minority students. However, Justice Powell's tie-breaking opinion in that case indicated that universities *could* instead consider race holistically—as one of a complex bundle of characteristics—if they argued that doing so benefits all students on campus by creating a diverse learning environment. Doing so would advance a compelling state interest—diverse classrooms—hence could be permissible under the Equal Protection Clause as long as it could pass strict scrutiny—that is, there were no other viable alternatives to affirmative action that did not consider race. Justice Powell's opinion accepting the "diversity rationale" provided universities a template for how to defend their affirmative action policies in the future.[17]

Since the *Bakke* decision, conservative and libertarian individuals and organizations have poured funding into additional anti–affirmative action lawsuits as well as ballot initiatives and state legislation around the country.[18] As a result, four more anti-affirmative action in higher education cases have landed in the US Supreme Court, with each decision affirming the diversity rationale.[19] In the 2016 *Fisher v. University of Texas* decision, the US Supreme Court upheld University of Texas's affirmative action program, but the justices also made clear that universities will no longer be afforded "good faith" understanding that they have tried other, race-neutral alternatives to achieve their diversity goals before turning to race. Instead, they will be expected by the court to be able to demonstrate that effort when questioned.

In the latest pair of cases being considered by the US Supreme Court, Asian Americans and whites represented by Students for Fair Admissions, or SFFA, have claimed they experienced racial discrimination in being denied admission to Harvard and University of North Carolina, Chapel Hill.[20] They cite as evidence the higher average GPAs and SAT scores of Asian American and white students admitted compared to other race groups. SFFA's proposed remedy in both cases is an end to all considerations of race in admissions, which means the end of affirmative action. A man named Edward Blum financed and recruited plaintiffs in the two cases, just as he did in the 2016 *Fisher v. Texas* case. Blum has also financed more recent lawsuits at Yale and University of Texas (again).[21] The Harvard and UNC Chapel Hill cases will be heard as this book goes to press. Given Justice Ketanji Brown Jackson's recusal because of her position on Harvard's Board of Overseers and Donald Trump's appointment of three justices since the last affirmative action case in the US Supreme Court, there are six conservative justices and two liberals slated to make a decision.

But these cases are just one of many ways to understand affirmative action. In this book, rather than restrict the discussion of affirmative action to the legal landscape, I take a broader approach, drawing from philosophy and especially from social science research. As a sociologist I rely on data to make sense of the world, and in the next chapter I do just that. I use data to analyze the benefits and potential drawbacks of affirmative action, all in the context of the purposes of higher education. The diverse goals and constituencies in universities create much of the confusion, conflict, and division around affirmative action, as we'll see. Divergent understandings of the role that race continues to play in the contemporary United States play a role, as well.

CHAPTER 2

The Case For and Against Affirmative Action

Just as the goals of admissions are diverse and complex, so too are the arguments supporting and critiquing affirmative action. Not surprisingly, given the myriad purposes of higher education, advocates and critics alike have identified multiple reasons for their views. In this chapter I highlight key arguments and consider how those arguments align with the university purposes outlined in the previous chapter. While the diversity rationale is the sole argument accepted by the US Supreme Court, I discuss other common arguments as well, and where those arguments have appeared.

Affirmative Action Creates Diverse Learning Environments

Recall that in multiple cases the US Supreme Court has agreed that considering race in admissions in order to create diverse learning environments is constitutional. This rationale contributes to the goal of teaching. Indeed, research continues to show that American political views and policy opinions are correlated with race, so racial diversity does broaden the perspectives present on campus.[1] Race differences in where people live, family structure, class, and experiences of racism also mean that racial diversity will broaden the lived experiences students bring to campus.

After Justice Powell first voiced acceptance for the diversity rationale in the 1978 *Bakke* decision, social scientists set out to understand just how—or if—diverse learning environments shape educational experiences and outcomes. We now know that a diverse student body provides considerable benefits to all students. Researchers have analyzed the relationship between a diverse student population and academic, civic, and attitudinal outcomes by tracking students across their college experiences and beyond. Most of these studies survey students at the beginning of college and after they have had some college experiences; some also study graduates. They then compare students with similar characteristics to each other, either on the same campus but with different levels of cross-racial interaction on campus, or students attending campuses with different levels of diversity, to see how diversity or cross-racial interaction on the same campus correlates with student outcomes.

This research has shown that a diverse student body makes students of *all* races more likely to discuss racial issues in college and to socialize with peers of other races, which in turn seems to improve educational outcomes (intellectual engagement, performance, and academic self-efficacy), self-perceived leadership capability, and self-confidence.[2] At the micro level, having a roommate of a different race is associated with lower levels of racial prejudice.[3] Beyond college, previous experience in a diverse student body is associated in adulthood with having more positive racial attitudes, diverse friendships, greater civic engagement, and stronger leadership skills.[4] These outcomes suggest that affirmative action supports the university purpose of contributing to society, given the positive impacts it seems to have on graduates.

These empirically proven benefits to all students on campus justify affirmative action legally as a mechanism to improve the overall learning environment. Indeed, given the well-documented benefits of diversity for educational outcomes and society writ large alongside the US Supreme Court's acceptance of the diversity rationale, selective colleges have embraced this argument.

Affirmative Action Benefits Society

The diversity rationale suggests that affirmative action benefits society through improving the racial attitudes, cognitive and leadership capacity, and civic participation of all students on campus. Relatedly, some have pointed out that affirmative action more directly benefits society as a whole. Economists Caroline Hoxby and Christopher Avery point to society's lost talent when disadvantaged kids do not reach their full potential—we have fewer doctors, scientists, and entrepreneurs to better society.[5] Others point out that leadership lacking representation will not be seen as legitimate by those who are not represented, so creating a pipeline to diverse leadership through affirmative action helps governance. This was one of the arguments made by Justice Sandra Day O'Connor in the 2003 *Grutter v. Bollinger* case. She argued that lack of diversity in leadership in society would delegitimize that leadership in the minds of many citizens. That is, national unity and effective governance required that people of all racial groups see themselves in the leadership of the country, which signals that people like them are included. Indeed, former President Barack Obama and US Supreme Court Justice Sonia Sotomayor have both pointed to affirmative action as enabling their social position; their presence in government has played an important role in signaling that leadership will be empathetic to the concerns of racial minorities.[6]

Affirmative action is also effective at increasing diversity among professionals, such as doctors, lawyers, and teachers. The need for diversity in the professions seems self-evident. We know from research that is two decades old, for example, that children do better in school when they have teachers who look like them.[7] Research on patient outcomes by race shows that Black patients benefit from Black doctors.[8] Black judges have been found to exhibit less implicit racial bias than white judges, which affects their decision-making.[9] The list goes on.

Indeed, affirmative action has proven effective at diversifying the pool of graduates from selective colleges who can go on to professional vocations. One study found that Black graduates of selective colleges went on to earn advanced degrees in large numbers, despite having lower average SAT scores than their white peers on campus, earning lower grades in high school than their peers on average, and coming from families with fewer economic resources.[10] Black students in the study were more likely to graduate when they attended higher-status colleges, and hence to go on to earn advanced degrees. Another study found that the 1998 end to affirmative action in California by referendum led to a decline in Black and Latinx graduates in STEM fields at University of California colleges.[11] In other words, despite slightly weaker academic training when they enter college, Black and Latinx students benefiting from affirmative action likely enter the professions in higher numbers as a result of it. Overall, the vast data on the benefits of diversity for society makes clear that affirmative action works to enhance our shared social life. And the impact of affirmative action on that diversity is clear from studies of graduates of selective colleges.

Affirmative Action Fosters Equal Opportunity

Most Americans—red and blue, rich and poor—care deeply about equal opportunity. If we all have roughly the same chances to reach the top, the argument goes, then the living conditions of those at the bottom are less of a concern because those in that position are assumed to deserve their position, just as those at the top are thought to deserve *their* position.[12] Given our commitments to equal opportunity, affirmative action is a way to level the playing field, serving as a correction for racial inequality in the United States. This justification aligns with the university purpose of facilitating equal opportunity and social mobility. Indeed, when colleges first began considering race in admissions, it was solely for this purpose.[13]

Students and college administrators in the US seem to agree that attention to opportunity should play a central role in admissions. When I interviewed Ivy League students about their views on college admissions for my book *The Diversity Bargain*, most told me that applicants should be evaluated in the context of opportunities they have had (and just as importantly, haven't had). So, for example, an applicant who took and did well on the only two Advanced Placement courses offered at her high school should be rated higher than another who took and did well in four of the ten offered at a different, better-resourced high school. Colleges, too, agree with this practice—Harvard admissions Dean William Fitzsimmons tells applicants, "We are vitally interested in whether or not applicants have taken full advantage of their educational opportunities, whatever they might have been," and Brown University's website tells applicants, "We know that curricular offerings vary from school to school. Our strongest candidates have taken full advantage of what is available to them in their own schools."[14]

With our deep-set belief in equal opportunity, the need for affirmative action rests on whether applicants of different races have equal opportunities to achieve what is required for admission. If race were not tied to opportunities, we would not need to consider race in order to give everyone a fair shot. But that is not the case; race shapes the extent to which Americans have opportunities in life. While a person's social class does impact their opportunities, educational and otherwise, all of our typical measures of class—whether parents attended a four-year college, household income, and even zip code—are still incapable of fully capturing opportunity differences by race. In other words, race plays an enduring role in Americans' material well-being apart from class.

Take the example of housing segregation: decades after the end of slavery, redlining policies during the 1920s meant the US government provided first-time homeowner loans only in neighborhoods inaccessible to African Americans because of legal segregation, effectively excluding them from loans to promote social mobility via property ownership.[15] Political scientist Ira Katznelson aptly describes this as a time "When Affirmative Action Was White."[16] The ongoing racial segregation today stemmed from those century-old policies.[17] Even after legal residential segregation ended half a century ago with the passage of the Fair Housing Act, considerable evidence suggests that people of color continue to face racial discrimination when trying to buy a home.[18]

Property ownership is far more than a home; it is a mechanism for wealth accumulation across generations, and partially explains dramatic differences in wealth by race in the United States.[19] This happens, for example, when parents with wealth provide support for a home down payment to their adult children, much more common in the white middle class compared to the Black middle class.[20] Today, the average white family holds over $170,000 in net assets, compared to just $17,000 for Black families, a tenfold difference.[21] As a result, Black and Latinx children grow up in higher poverty, lower-income neighborhoods than white and Asian American children.[22] Even middle-class Black families tend to live in more disadvantaged neighborhoods compared to whites of the same social class.[23] Housing is also tied to educational quality, because local taxes pay for most of the costs of public education in the United States.[24] And our schools remain stubbornly segregated by race. Even poor white children, as a result of these trends, tend to attend schools with higher levels of achievement than the schools attended by poor Black and Latinx children.[25]

US higher education also has a long history of segregation. Southern colleges resisted educating white and Black students together well into the second half of the twentieth century, and did so by sending Black students out of state for higher education, creating poorly funded Black colleges, and segregating Black students in separate, unequal classrooms.[26] Northern colleges admitted a token few Black students to demonstrate they were not exclusively white, but admissions requirements meant that very few Black students could even consider applying to those colleges. That stratified foundation means that previously segregated white colleges now have substantial endowments and donor bases that fund campus facilities, the recruitment of top faculty, and more, while many historically Black colleges and universities (HBCUs) continue to operate under severe financial precarity.[27]

Beyond segregation, decades of research has also shown that unequal opportunities continue to shape the educational experiences of Black, Latinx, and Native American youth, even within the same schools, and even with well-meaning teachers. To take one example, when tested for unconscious bias, most teachers show pro-white, anti-Black bias.[28] In turn, a teacher's implicit racial bias is associated with worse teaching and learning outcomes for their Black students.[29] Black youth also experience more disciplinary surveillance at school and harsher punishments than their white peers, even for the same infractions.[30] These unequal experiences in school are compounded for those Black and Latinx students who do get to college, because they are less likely to have college-educated parents than their white peers, making them less than half as likely to complete a bachelor's degree.[31] Relatedly, Black and Latinx college students tend to attend lower-status colleges than white college students, another factor that drives down completion rates and leads to divergent post-college outcomes.[32]

These differences make for different educational outcomes prior to college, for which affirmative action might serve as a useful corrective. For example, the SAT is highly correlated with race and household income.[33] Beyond academics, the gap between what well-off and lower-income parents are spending on their children's extracurricular activities has been steadily growing over time.[34] It is easy to assume that sports recruiting provides opportunities to poor kids of color from underperforming urban schools. If this were the norm, then sports recruiting could be an engine of social mobility and racial equity. However, more often than not, recruited student athletes come from white families with deep pockets.[35]

The ongoing impact of our history of racial exclusion seems undeniable, and thus, proponents of affirmative action argue, if we are serious about our ideal of equal opportunity, we must pay attention to race, in college admissions and elsewhere. Still, despite equal opportunity being the first central impetus for affirmative action in higher education, and the plethora of evidence that race plays a role in opportunities, the US Supreme Court has not permitted attention to race to create a level playing field as a justification for affirmative action. As a result, in recent decades colleges have mostly stayed away from arguments highlighting racial equity as a justification for affirmative action.[36] I turn next to an important—but often overlooked—justification for affirmative action: reparations.

Affirmative Action Is an Important Form of Reparations

Beyond leveling the playing field, we might consider affirmative action as a form of compensation for past wrongs, or reparations. Affirmative action as reparations is not a commonly expressed justification, and it has not been upheld in court. Still, I present the case here because when we consider the harms done to particular minority groups, the moral case for reparations is clear (Of course, the lack of alignment with a specific goal of universities may explain why this idea has not taken hold). A handful of intellectuals of color have indeed argued that we should consider affirmative action as one form of reparations.[37]

For decades, both in Congress and beyond, some politicians and intellectuals have argued for reparations to African Americans.[38] The idea gained momentum after the murder of George Floyd in 2020. That year, the city of Evanston, Illinois, pledged $10 million in housing grants to individuals who could prove that they or their ancestors experienced housing discrimination in the city.[39] In 2021 the US House of Representatives Judiciary Committee recommended a commission on reparations for African Americans.[40]

Native Americans have also been harmed by US expansionist policies. While the Indian Claims Commission, established in 1946, provided some financial compensation to Native American tribes, the amounts paid were paltry compared to the wrongs done, and do not preclude affirmative action as further compensation. The possibilities for reparations are even broader. US expansionism wreaked havoc on indigenous peoples, but it has also harmed Latinx communities. In the southwest of the United States,

Mexican residents were forcibly incorporated into the United States as a result of the Mexican American War; further east, Puerto Rico was colonized by the United States after the Spanish American War. In recent decades, as well, the ascent of neoliberalism—epitomized by the North American Free Trade Agreement and similar policies, under which wages suffer because companies and farmers in developing countries often cannot compete with large US multinational firms—fuels economic precarity throughout Latin America and drives migration to the US.[41] Considering this history, group-based reparations may be one way to account for past systematic harms toward African Americans and other people of color in the United States and around the world.

We know that elite colleges in the United States in particular have benefited from racial exclusion and exploitation. An investigation by Brown University revealed that the founders of the university benefited from the slave trade, used profits from slavery to establish the university, and forced enslaved laborers to construct university buildings.[42] Brown, of course, is far from alone; in one way or another, nearly all elite colleges have benefited from slave labor or profits from the slave trade, or from US expansionism and neoliberalism more generally.[43]

College admission can be one form of reparations, whether to specific individuals whose ancestors were harmed by the racist acts of a specific college, or to groups excluded from and exploited by the university or American society overall. In 2016 Georgetown University announced it would implement reparations in admissions for the descendants of slaves whose labor and sale helped maintain the university.[44] Under the plan, applicants to Georgetown who are the descendants of those slaves receive a leg up in admission, just as children of alumni do. Of course, a boost in admission does not preclude other important forms of reparations, such as cash assistance, as Georgetown is also doing.[45] Beyond individual descendants of people harmed by individual colleges, we might consider affirmative action more generally as a mechanism to provide reparations to African Americans, Native Americans, and Latinx for the harms of racial exclusion in the United States overall, of which all selective colleges were a part.[46]

We now have a half century of research that leaves no doubt: affirmative action works. By any—and all—of these four measures, affirmative action is the right thing to do. The intended beneficiaries do indeed seem to gain from it, whether underrepresented minority or white, as does our society as a whole. It advances the university goals of furthering equal opportunity, teaching, and contributing to society. Still, it is important to remember that the equity and reparations justifications have not been accepted by the US Supreme Court. They are thus vulnerable to white (and Asian American) claims of racial discrimination, because the court has not accepted arguments about group-based harm and opportunity. As a result, selective colleges have largely abandoned discussion of equity as a justification for affirmative action, in favor of the diversity rationale. This turn protects them legally and has spilled over into the overall language used around diversity and race.[47]

Given the compelling evidence above for affirmative action, why is the consideration of race in college admissions so controversial? I turn next to critiques of affirmative action.

Affirmative Action Is Racial Discrimination

The most common critique of affirmative action is deceivingly simple: that it amounts to racial discrimination against whites and Asian Americans. According to this argument, providing a leg up to underrepresented groups means less opportunities for other groups, because college admissions is a zero-sum game—if you provide greater accommodation for a certain group of people, that means there are fewer slots available to every other group of people. This is the argument made in each of the cases that have made it to the US Supreme Court, and it aligns with conservative and libertarian activists' goal of eliminating all attention to racial inequality, whether in college admissions, examining changes to voting laws, or even sharing empirical evidence of racial inequality and injustice in schools.[48] These activists frequently employ the language of civil rights to make this argument.[49] Rather than relying on social science data on the alignment between affirmative action and university goals, this argument takes a colorblind liberal individualist approach, assuming individual autonomy and equal opportunities as the bedrock of American society (it ignores, of course, the ways that racial inequality and racism impede equal opportunity and individual autonomy).

These critics often argue that attention to race, whether to discriminate *against* one group or to provide opportunities *for* another group, is wrong no matter the rationale. They claim that affirmative action creates undue harm toward whites and Asian Americans. They also sometimes express concern that affirmative action may reify race in harmful ways. That is, affirmative action may draw undue attention to race, perpetuating racial stereotypes and racial division. Affirmative action could end up hurting, rather than helping, racial minorities and, more broadly, a society that is trying to move beyond past racial divisions.

Other opponents admit of the possibility that affirmative action might have been justified in the past but think that it is no longer necessary, and that now the harm to whites and Asian Americans is greater than any of the potential benefits. Despite the evidence (summarized above), many Americans believe that racial inequality no longer plays a role in the opportunities each individual has. Often this belief is justified by a colorblindness view—that is, a belief that race does not play a significant role in social life, and that any race differences that exist can be explained by other means, such as class (lack of economic resources), or culture (different behaviors, values, or work ethic, for example).[50] They point to the economic disadvantages that poor whites and poor people of color have in common, as well as the common disadvantages experienced by children whose parents lack a college degree, regardless of their race. Critics who attribute race differences to economic resources often support class-based considerations in college admission (for example, giving preference to certain class groups, or to certain zip codes), but not affirmative action.[51] These critics sometimes assume that affirmative action and class-based considerations are locked in competition—they assume that colleges must pick one or the other. Of course, there is no reason to believe that they must. Indeed, attention to class-based diversity on elite college campuses has grown in recent years, even as affirmative action has continued on many of those same campuses.

This argument is often used, too, to suggest that diversity, whether on campus or in companies, is unimportant, since race does not determine our perspectives on the world. As outlined above, however, considerable evidence suggests that measures of class—household income, parents' levels of education, median household income in an applicant's zip code—do not fully capture profound differences in opportunity, nor the racial divides in our lived experiences and political views.[52]

Some of these critics suggest that underrepresented groups simply do not aspire as much or work as hard, and hence are not deserving of affirmative action. However, empirical research has shown that different levels of ambition and grit do not explain different levels of achievement by race. In fact, children and parents of different races express remarkably similar beliefs about the importance of education.[53] Black middle-class parents spend just as much time fretting over where to live and how to cultivate their children's talents and agency as white parents do (they also fret about how to ensure their children's safety and find environments in which their children are not always the only Black child in the room).[54] In a school-wide survey at a diverse suburban school I found that Black students reported *more* pressure from their parents to do well in school than Asian American and white students did.[55]

In addition to critiquing the equal opportunity rationale for affirmative action, this perspective also clashes with the idea of reparations. Some whites and Asian Americans argue that because they (and in many cases, their ancestors) were not the individual perpetuators of racial disadvantage, they should not be denied opportunities due to affirmative action—in other words, they should not be asked as part of a collective to provide reparations for past harms committed by others. From this vantage point, Georgetown's reparations for the descendants of specific slaves makes sense, but not broader compensation for African Americans in general, which would be unfair to a few marginal white and Asian American applicants denied admission.

While it is tempting to take this individual approach, it is problematic. Most importantly, our ability to trace the biographies and descendants of individual slaves is extremely limited; most African Americans know little of their individual ancestors' ordeals, not to mention who benefited from their ancestors' labor. In fact, erasure of individual biographies and the separation of families was part and parcel of the institution of chattel slavery in the US south.[56] In fact, one critique of Georgetown's admissions preferences for descendants of slaves whose labor the university benefited from is that the policy did not allocate sufficient resources toward identifying and contacting those descendants.[57] Most universities have even fewer resources to put toward this kind of investment.

But the more fundamental problem with this approach is that it denies a basic reality of human existence: despite the longstanding American ideal of individualism, we often function and treat each other as members of groups. If we believe reparations should only be available to individuals whose ancestors were harmed explicitly (and, in turn, should only be paid by the descendants of the perpetrators of harm) we reject the reality of our group membership. We reject the reality that African Americans, as a community, have been harmed by racism and racial exclusion, and that whites, as a community, have benefited from racial exclusion. And the ongoing impact of racial exclusion affects all Black Americans, just as the privileges associated with being white accrue to all whites. In fact, research on racial attitudes has found that whites who feel a sense of "group threat" —that Black Americans are gaining ground too fast and leaving whites behind—are more likely to oppose policies like affirmative action; feelings of group threat correlate more strongly with opposition to affirmative action than do philosophical views about individualism.[58]

By now it should be clear that the empirical evidence does not support the claim of racial discrimination that opponents of affirmative action make. The argument makes the mistake of viewing college admissions as an individualist meritocracy that evaluates individuals out of the context of documented racial inequality in American society. What's clear is that these arguments are part of a broader conservative and libertarian agenda to move toward a colorblind society that ignores evidence of racial inequality or discrimination. Moreover, these voices fail to consider the ways that affirmative action can further university goals of contributing to society, promoting equal opportunity, and excellence in teaching.

Affirmative Action Creates Mismatch between Students and Their Universities

Some critics of affirmative action express concern that it will harm the presumed main beneficiaries—Black, Latinx, and Native American students who end up at colleges where they may have weaker academic skills than many of their white and Asian American peers. That is, affirmative action may get them in over their heads. Richard Sander and Stuart Taylor make this argument in their book, *Mismatch.* They argue that affirmative action makes Black and Latinx students less likely to major in STEM fields and to graduate, because of mismatch.[59]

While this may seem a more empathetic take on affirmative action—wanting what is best for under-represented minority students—empirical data simply does not support the claim of mismatch.[60] Bowen and Bok's early study of affirmative action, *The Shape of the River,* showed that Black students admitted to selective colleges via affirmative action were more likely to go on to attain advanced degrees than if they had attended colleges where their SAT scores were closer to the average on campus. Among even Black students whose SAT score placed them in the lowest level for selective colleges (below 1000 out of 1600), the higher-status college they attended the more likely they were to graduate. Further, these students went on to earn more than comparably prepared students (as measured by SAT score) who attended lower-status colleges.[61] These outcomes are likely a result of higher-status universities having more resources to support students and overall higher rates of graduation, which benefits all students on those campuses, including those admitted under affirmative action with weaker than average preparation prior to college.[62] Just as we frequently assume admissions is all about individual merit, and ignore the fact that admissions is about an institution's goals and commitments to the broader society, so too student outcomes appear to be more tied to the institutional environment—where they go to college—than to their individual achievements prior to college.

A more recent study of admissions to University of California before and after the 1998 ban came to similar conclusions.[63] Economist Zachary Bleemer found that underrepresented minority students were less likely to graduate college and to obtain a STEM degree *after* the ban; this was especially true for students with weaker academic preparation (those thought to be most negatively affected by "mismatch"). Wages for

Latinx graduates after college declined by five percent, as well.[64]

Still, proponents of mismatch theory point out that students benefiting from affirmative action are less likely to graduate than those with higher academic qualifications.[65] Indeed, the recent data from University of California shows this. However, the data also shows that affirmative action brought a greater number of Black and Latinx students to campus overall, which in turn led to a greater number of Black and Latinx graduates overall prior to the ban. These outcomes suggest that a significant number of students benefiting from affirmative action are indeed successful and attending higher-status universities at the very least did not diminish their likelihood of graduating.

The mismatch argument might hold true if the skills of students admitted under affirmative action were dramatically lower than their peers on campus, but the data suggest this is not the case. Mismatch theory seems to overestimate just how large the gap is between affirmative action students and everyone else. The data also suggest that there is a wider pool of students who could be successful at most colleges than those colleges have seats for. This means that each college can and should consider institutional goals and contributions to society in their admissions processes rather than simply selecting "top" students, who are not the only ones likely to be successful at the college and hence to support colleges in their institutional goals.[66]

Conclusion: The Importance of Affirmative Action

The cumulative data from over three decades of research on affirmative action is clear: the benefits of affirmative action are substantial, and little evidence exists for ending it. The data make clear that attention to diverse learning environments, contributions to society, racial equity, and reparations all warrant affirmative action. Further, when we free ourselves of the idea that admission is solely driven by individual achievement, and instead accept that admissions is part of the mission and institutional reality of colleges, affirmative action becomes even harder to critique.

As we have seen, the arguments against affirmative action center on the role of race in American society. Critics are reluctant to acknowledge the ongoing impact of racial exclusion. They suggest that race no longer plays a role in American society, apart from its correlation with class, an artifact of history that many assume will fade over time on its own. These critics prioritize an individualist perspective on admissions and fairness, rather than attention to group differences and group-based equity. But this argument perpetuates an inaccurate picture of life in the United States, minority experiences on elite college campuses, and the potential benefits of affirmative action, not just to underrepresented minorities, but also to white and Asian American students and to our society as a whole as well.

In fact, some advocates of affirmative action argue that the most common justification today, the diversity rationale, still privileges whites, because it emphasizes the benefits of diversity to *white* students' learning. Half a century ago legal scholar Derrick Bell developed his theory of "interest convergence," which hypothesized that civil rights victories would only be won only when the interests of those in power—whites—converged with the interests of those with less power—African Americans.[67] As evidence Bell cited the 1954 decision in *Brown v. Board of Education* as a victory that enabled US leadership to showcase racial justice in the United States at a time of growing US international power. Bell's prediction proved prescient when the US Supreme Court accepted the diversity rationale as a justification for affirmative action, but not the equal opportunity rationale. More recently, in my book *The Diversity Bargain* I demonstrate how white students continue to view affirmative action almost exclusively as a policy designed to benefit them; this leads those students to question Black, Latinx, and Native American peers who turn to each other for support, join minority student groups, and sit together in the cafeteria. It also makes them prone to holding "reverse discrimination" beliefs when they go on to apply to graduate school or jobs and are unsuccessful. In other words, the diversity rationale, more than the equal opportunity, contributions to society, and reparations arguments, treats college admissions as an individualist meritocracy in a colorblind society, with less focus on the other purposes of higher education that we have discussed throughout this book. Hence, it is critical to pay attention to all the rationales for affirmative action, even those rejected in court.

The use of anti-discrimination law as a mechanism to *prevent* attention to race in college admissions, as plaintiffs in affirmative action cases have done, can feel like an ironic twist to the goals of the Fourteenth Amendment and the Civil Rights Act, given their original focus on rights for African Americans. This ground becomes even murkier when we consider the case of Asian Americans. As a group, Asian Americans experience racial discrimination. At the same time, Asian American youth have experienced high levels of academic success on average, in part due to US immigration policy that has brought substantial numbers of highly skilled immigrants from Asia to the United States. Some have used the case of Asian Americans to claim that other racial minorities should not need affirmative action. Others even suggest that affirmative action amounts to racial discrimination toward Asian Americans. Why should one minority group suffer, the argument goes, due to preferences for others? However, as we'll see in the next chapter, this argument is deeply flawed.

CHAPTER 3

Asian Americans, Achievement, and Affirmative Action

In recent years, opponents of affirmative action have repeatedly pointed to Asian Americans as proof that affirmative action is unnecessary. They point to Asian Americans' remarkable academic achievement as evidence that racism no longer encumbers racial minorities in the United States. If Asian Americans can achieve academic success, the story goes, so too can other minority groups. To these critics, Asian American achievement is evidence that the United States has achieved equal opportunity with respect to race, and thus, that affirmative action is no longer necessary.

In addition, the SAT scores and high-school GPAs of Asian Americans on elite campuses—high even compared to their white classmates—suggest to some that Asian Americans are being discriminated against in college admissions, and that the proportion of Asian Americans admitted should be even higher. Not surprisingly, affirmative action usually takes the blame. Most recently, as we've seen, Edward Blum has funded anti-affirmative action lawsuits that feature Asian American plaintiffs.[1] Blum actively recruited Asian Americans to his cause, asking, in countless ads featuring Asian Americans, "Were you denied admission to Harvard/Yale/UNC/University of Wisconsin-Madison? It may be because you're the wrong race." Some Asian American anti-affirmative action activists share this view and have joined forces with Blum.[2]

But does Asian American academic achievement truly mean affirmative action is unnecessary, and may even be unfair?

Asian Americans offer us a unique vantage point on affirmative action. Because we exist outside the Black-white binary, and because we upset the typical assumptions of how a minority group achieves, examining Asian Americans helps dig deeper into the messiness of affirmative action and arguments related to it. Here I want to explore the justifications for affirmative action and the racial discrimination argument against it (but not mismatch, which is relevant only to students benefiting directly from affirmative action). For each one I ask: "Does Asian American academic achievement suggest affirmative action should not continue, based on this justification?" As we'll see, different histories of slavery, migration, and US politics have facilitated Asian American academic achievement, and dampened it for other racial minorities. Ultimately, I argue that

Asian American achievement does not undermine the arguments for affirmative action. Still, I point out that if discrimination toward Asian Americans in admissions does exist, steps should be taken to address that discrimination; ending affirmative action is not the solution to any anti-Asian American discrimination, past or present.

Asian Americans and the Diversity Rationale

Fostering more diverse learning environments on elite college campuses requires affirmative action to bolster the numbers of Black, Latinx, and Native American students on campus. This consideration, absent increases in enrollment, requires a small decrease in the number of white and Asian American students admitted, and is justified given the extensive research cited in Chapter 2. Still, while Indian Americans, Chinese Americans, and Korean Americans are particularly well-represented on selective college campuses, some Asian American groups, like Laotian Americans and Hmong Americans, are not. Hence, using affirmative action to bring their distinct voices to a campus seems a worthy consideration given the diversity rationale.

Some might argue that the large numbers of Asian Americans on some selective college campuses detracts from a diverse learning environment. However, this should not matter, given that on almost all selective campuses whites, not Asian Americans, are the largest race group (notable exceptions are California Institute of Technology, and University of California, Berkeley). Thus, limiting the percentage of Asian American students to make room for more white students does not address the goal of a diverse learning environment, so it is not justified. To argue otherwise is to play into harmful essentializing of Asian Americans as "all the same" while acknowledging the diverse life experiences of whites. In fact, there are greater class differences among Asian Americans than any other race group in the United States.[3] Creating a diverse learning environment means addressing *under*-representation, not limiting the presence of minority groups that have a larger proportion of students on campus than others.

Asian Americans and the Social Contributions Justification

How do Asian Americans fit into the goal of bettering society? If one goal of affirmative action is to develop a quorum of potential leaders from all racial groups, then Asian Americans should not qualify, since we are well-represented on selective college campuses already. On the other hand, Asian American academic success does not preclude affirmative action for other racial minorities to diversify leadership and, overall, to better American society.

Still, it is important to recognize that Asian Americans are underrepresented in leadership positions in the corporate sector, government, and the media.[4] However, given the number of Asian Americans graduating from selective colleges, the problem seems to be downstream. In government and the media, attracting more Asian Americans to those fields after college may increase representation. In the corporate sector, research has shown that Asian Americans frequently face "bamboo ceilings" that prevent them from entering the top levels of private sector firms.[5] This is an important social problem, but not one that more Asian Americans on elite college campuses is likely to solve.

Asian Americans, the Equal Opportunity Justification, and the Racial Discrimination Critique

One of the central arguments for affirmative action, as we have seen, is that opportunity in the United States is unequal; those who oppose affirmative action insist, however, that race no longer shapes our opportunities. Some of these opponents argue that Asian American academic success is the perfect demonstration that opportunity is open to anyone, and is proof that we have overcome racial inequality. Thus, the argument goes, if Black and Latinx families fall behind it must be the result of lack of motivation, or a different work ethic or cultural practices, in contrast to "model minority" Asian Americans, whose success shows how to be a "good" minority in America.[6]

Does Asian American academic achievement indeed prove that equal opportunity does exist? If not, how do we explain why Asian American kids are now routinely outperforming all other groups academically—even their white peers? Many describe the model minority idea as a myth, a simplistic concept that ignores the historical realities and social policies that have enabled material success for a large percentage of Asian Americans, and denied it for a large percentage of African Americans, Latinx, and Native Americans.[7]

US immigration policy along with the massive US border with Mexico, in fact, have played a large role in ethnic differences in achievement. A majority of Latin American immigrants have arrived through low-skilled migration, both authorized and unauthorized. As a result, over eighty percent of Mexican immigrants in the United States have less than a high school education.[8] In contrast, the 1965 Hart-Celler Act enabled highly skilled immigrants to come to the United States from, among other places, Asia. As a result, trained doctors, nurses, engineers, and scientists—especially from China, India, the Philippines, and Korea—have come to work in American hospitals, engineering firms, and more.[9] Relatedly, today over half of Indian and Chinese immigrants—the two largest Asian immigrant groups in the US—have at least a bachelor's degree.[10]

These structural realities have shaped vastly different trajectories for these two groups. A large percentage of Asian immigrants are highly skilled and bring with them cultural know-how for excelling in academics (especially on standardized tests, which were the backbone of their educational success in Asia). In other words, US immigration policy means that most Asian immigrants have strong skills for doing well on academic tests—that is what enabled them to come to the United States in the first place. And they pass those skills on to their children, who consequently also excel academically compared to all other race groups, including whites, especially in standardized testing.[11] Some insist that Asians simply value education more than other minority groups, but the real story of Asian American achievement has to do with US immigration policy, alongside expansionism, centuries of slavery and exclusion of African Americans, and the persistent reliance on low-skilled labor from Latin America.

Given the class standing of most Asian Americans, many actually benefit from social policies designed to exclude African Americans. Sociologists Tukufu Zuberi and Eduardo Bonilla-Silva have shown how educational testing was developed by psychologists intent on proving the superiority of whites over people of color; many of those early thinkers were self-proclaimed eugenicists.[12] Once this system was in place, highly skilled Asian immigrants came to the United States and drew from their skills developed in Asia to help their children excel on standardized tests like the SAT and entrance exams to elite public schools like Stuyvesant High School in New York, mechanisms that have historically shut Black and Latinx youth out of elite educational opportunities. In addition, Asian Americans have benefited from the history of racial segregation in housing. As we have seen, racial exclusion enabled well-educated whites to congregate in upper-middle-class suburbs around the country, and to pool their property taxes into excellent schools that did not have to spend money on the needs of children from less resourced families.[13] Today,

Asian Americans suffer less racial discrimination in the housing market and this, along with their high levels of education and a decline in explicit racial exclusion, has enabled many Asian American professionals to move into those same suburbs that used to be predominantly white. These two factors—success on standardized testing and residence in upper-middle-class suburbs— have enabled many professional Asian immigrants to experience the American dream more easily and more often than other minority groups.[14]

Despite educational and economic success, it is important to recognize that Asian Americans do face racism and racial stereotypes. During the nineteenth century, when the United States began restricting immigration, Asian immigrants were the first targets, excluded long before eastern, southern, and Jewish Europeans were. Further, Asian Americans were barred from US citizenship until well into the twentieth century, and Japanese Americans were interned during World War II. Today, anti-Asian hate crimes are on the rise, fueled in part by associations with the coronavirus and negative stereotypes about Muslims.[15] Some argue that since Asian Americans experience racism, too, then racism should not prevent African Americans from succeeding. However, critical differences exist between anti-Asian and anti-Black racism.

While Asian Americans are frequently stereotyped as foreign and emotionally cold, we are also stereotyped as competent.[16] That particular bundle of assumptions leads to a phenomenon called "stereotype promise," in which educators assume competence and hold Asian American youth to high expectations.[17] Decades of research in education shows that high expectations are the key to high performance in children, so stereotype promise can actually bolster Asian American achievement. In contrast, African Americans are often stereotyped as warm but lacking competence, including with respect to academic achievement.[18] This particular bundle can lead to the opposite phenomenon—"stereotype threat"—in which African Americans may fear living up to a negative stereotype, and consequently underperform on, for example, academic assessments.[19] Low academic expectations in school are also known to harm Black children's achievement.[20] Thus Asian Americans can and do face racism and racial stereotypes, but that treatment does not normally impede their academic achievement (and indeed, may sometimes even help it); instead, it harms their ability to be seen as American (and sometimes to be promoted to managerial positions).[21]

Where does this complex story of opportunities and racial exclusion leave Asian Americans with respect to affirmative action's goal of equal opportunity? The majority who have benefited from highly educated parents, life in well-resourced neighborhoods, and above-average household incomes should not be afforded a leg up through affirmative action. But the minority of Asian Americans, whose families arrived as refugees due to US involvement in foreign wars—for example, Hmong Americans—should indeed qualify for affirmative action. Under this form of implementation, affirmative action does indeed address unequal opportunities, and hence is justified.

The role of race in the lives of Asian Americans is undeniable—the dramatic rise in anti-Asian hate crimes is the most obvious evidence of that role—and yet, when it comes to educational opportunities race does not harm most Asian Americans the way it has harmed other racial minorities. Other solutions are needed to address anti–Asian American racism, and affirmative action for less advantaged racial minorities makes sense when we consider the different histories of each group.

Asian Americans and the Reparations Justification

Similar to the equal opportunity justification, reparations seems applicable to just a small portion of Asian

Americans. While Asian Americans undoubtedly suffer from racial stereotypes, we have not faced the same pervasive exclusion as other minority groups; and in some cases, Asian stereotypes can actually improve academic achievement. There is a small but significant caveat: US interventions in foreign wars suggest a role for reparations for some Asian Americans, such as Vietnamese refugees and their descendants. Aside from those groups, the historical record does not lend itself to reparations for Asian Americans, and it does not reduce the need for reparations for other minority groups, either.

Conclusion: The Complexities of Race

Just as affirmative action is nuanced and complex, so too is race. In practice, this point is painfully obvious; yet too often our understanding of race still gets stuck in the Black-white binary.[22] We must move beyond that binary and—in this instance—acknowledge that affirmative action does not apply to every minority group in the same way. That fact is not evidence for the policy's failure, but rather evidence of the complexity of race and racism's varied intrusions upon our lives. The discussion in this chapter suggests that affirmative action, if implemented to increase the numbers of Black, Latinx, and Native American students on campus (and some Asian American groups), remains an important admissions practice when we examine the case of Asian Americans.

The fact that Asian Americans are racial minorities who suffer from racism and racial stereotypes does not automatically mean we should benefit from affirmative action; nor does it mean we should be exempt from making room for underrepresented groups. Indeed, we need to have a more nuanced understanding of how racial stereotypes pigeon-hole groups differently. In addition, as we have explored, attention to equal opportunity must also consider the histories of migration, foreign policy, immigration policy, and racial exclusion to determine whether a group should qualify for affirmative action under the four justifications. Most Asian Americans would not qualify, and the policy does not hamper their own success when implemented for other minority groups.

It is possible, in fact, that Asian Americans experience racial stereotyping in the college admissions process; evidence from the *SFFA v. Harvard* trial showed small disparities, for example, in school guidance counselors' personal ratings of Asian Americans compared to other groups.[23] If future evidence suggests that this minor difference was not a coincidence, steps should be taken to reduce that anti-Asian bias. However, ending affirmative action would not resolve this issue, as plaintiffs in that trial have suggested it would. Anti-bias training, for example, is a more obvious possibility to reduce anti-Asian racial bias.

Still, high levels of achievement among Asian Americans should not be used as a justification for privileging white applicants over Asian Americans. Consider the four justifications for affirmative action: none requires admitting whites over Asian Americans with similar qualifications. Asian Americans do not have additional opportunities compared to whites of the same social class. They certainly have not benefited from Black exclusion more than whites. Nor would privileging white over Asian American applicants further university goals of teaching, research, or furthering the public good. Lastly, whites are more represented in leadership across sectors than Asian Americans.

The very public trial of *SFFA v. Harvard* has placed Asian Americans front and center in discussions of affirmative action, given the claim of anti-Asian discrimination rooted in affirmative action. I hope by now it has become clear that affirmative action does not *cause* anti-Asian American bias, nor can it *end* that bias. We need creative strategies to tackle racial stereotypes that have become increasingly dangerous for Asian Americans, and bias that may appear in teacher evaluations. However, ending affirmative action cannot do so. And the evidence makes clear that Asian American academic success does not demonstrate the presence of equal opportunity for all people of color, either. Affirmative action ensures that the playing field of college admissions is more level, and that a broad range of voices are heard on college campuses and beyond. As such, it serves the university missions of contributions to individual advancement and to our society as a whole. Asian American achievement does not change that.

From Fairness to Justice

Despite the legal attacks on affirmative action, I hope the evidence in this book has convinced you, as it has me, that it is a worthy policy. Universities should double down on the consideration of race in admissions and find new strategies for defending it legally. We can also see the fundamental value of this practice by looking at its absence: in states that have banned affirmative action, we see decreases in representation in higher education and even in future wages for under-represented minorities.[1] If this were to extend to the rest of the country and all selective private universities, we would in turn see a reduction in the numbers of doctors, teachers, CEOs, elected officials, and other prominent roles in society filled by African Americans, Native Americans, and Latinx—a particularly painful step backwards, especially considering the increasing diversity in American society.

Affirmative action promotes justice, at both the individual and group levels. It enhances the purposes of the university in being a force for good by providing more equitable opportunities by race. It improves the learning experiences of all students on campus, including white and Asian American students. It begins to account for the centuries of exploitation of individuals who are Black, Latinx, and Native American, and acknowledges that this history continues to shape social life today. During the 1960s some universities began to institute affirmative action out of desires to land on the right side of justice and equity, and to be seen as leaders in the fight for racial justice. Today, as the United States reckons with ongoing racial injustice, as we keep learning about new ways that implicit racial bias shapes the life opportunities of Black Americans, and as eleven million immigrants continue to live unauthorized without basic rights, I believe that all universities should feel that commitment as urgently as many of their predecessors did more than a half century ago.

But we also need to revise our understanding of college admissions itself. Nearly all of us see the admissions process as an individualist, meritocratic competition. This is the wrong way to look at it. College admission is not and should not be an evaluation of the worthiness of individuals. Rather, it should be a way for universities to fulfill their missions, which are most often related to contributing to our shared social world. This means we need greater representation to make sure our future leaders are exposed to diverse perspectives and lived experiences, and that our future leadership is seen as legitimate. In addition, colleges in the United States are embedded in a society plagued by rampant inequality, including racial inequality, and one in which we often turn to education as a mechanism to address that inequality. As such, affirmative action is one necessary policy. The lack of clarity on university purposes allows families to map their own meaning onto selection, as certifying merit. Universities should correct those misunderstandings by foregrounding and making explicit their goals when they discuss admissions.

Of course, affirmative action is not enough to fully address the diverse goals of our universities. Moreover, its impact may be paltry compared to both government and private universities simply *doing more to help more people*: increasing financial aid, increasing funding for state and community colleges, increasing funding for historically Black colleges and universities, increasing social supports for working class and poor families, increasing the minimum wage, changing tax policies to redistribute economic resources, and so much more. But these policies are not zero sum—we should pursue them alongside affirmative action, not as a replacement. Supporting affirmative action does not preclude supporting an expansion of other provisions to increase equity, nor the reverse. We need many tools to chip away at the vast problem of social inequality.

Still, affirmative action matters, for all the reasons I have outlined in this book. And it holds symbolic value, especially when instituted by the most elite colleges. When places like Harvard—synonymous in our popular imagination with excellence and meritocracy—back affirmative action it affirms both that racial exclusion is real, and that there is something we can (and should) do to fight it. And often, because colleges tend to look upward when comparing themselves to other colleges, when Harvard acts many others will follow its lead.[2]

As we confront the inherent murkiness of college admissions, it is clear that there are countless answers to the question of the "best" way to admit students. There is no perfect, most fair constellation of considerations for admission. Reasonable people will disagree. And even if we agree on the criteria, reasonable people will disagree on how to measure those criteria. They cater to different goals of universities, too. In other words, college admissions will never be a completely "fair" "objective" system. Instead, we should view college admissions as an imperfect system in which universities must make decisions in a world of unequal opportunities and imperfect information about what students' future trajectories will be, and in light of multiple purposes of their organizations. And it should certainly not be seen as a system of reward for individual achievement. As such, as I have argued throughout this book, "fairness" is the wrong way to analyze affirmative action.

The Way Forward

I hope I have convinced you that we cannot talk about affirmative action without first considering the goals of a university (even if many of the people arguing against affirmative action have no interest in doing so). If you are a college administrator and agree with the arguments in this book, then I urge you to consider your university's mission, and how you might tie your selection decisions to that mission. If that mission does not seem to align with the university's work and admissions policies, the first step is not to focus on the little details (like whether to require SAT scores), but instead to focus on the big picture (what is your university trying to do in the first place?). Once that mission is clear, greater transparency in those goals and how admissions ties to them may calm the nerves of many a high school senior and their parents. And for all of you who are *not* a college administrator but who are connected to this issue in some other way—as a parent of a college-aged kid, or as someone with an ideological disagreement with affirmative action, or as an activist who thinks affirmative action should push further, or as a college student yourself—I think this discussion is just as relevant for you. We all have a role to play in shifting our shared understanding of how college admissions works, and what it means to get admitted to a particular university.

I think we need to begin—both college administrators and all the rest of us with skin in this game —by reconsidering the value (and the impacts) of all the various ways that colleges choose students. Consider old assumptions: for example, should we keep our college cohort sizes, given that the number of eighteen-year-olds, the number of applicants, and the number of high achievers on the SAT have all dramatically increased over the past half century?[3] How many international students should we admit compared to domestic students, and why? Do we value sports teams enough to continue athletic recruiting, and at the current scale? Should we do the same for the orchestra? Do we value multigenerational legacy families enough to maintain the current level of preference for legacy applicants? To what end?

We know that all selective colleges, even the most elite ones, look at the same basic things as they conduct a "holistic review" of each applicant: SAT scores (though these are increasingly optional), grade point averages, letters of recommendation from teachers, student essays, listings of extracurricular achievements, and athletic excellence. In addition, many selective colleges look at financial need in at least some of their admissions decisions so that they can balance their books. Many also consider whether an applicant's family has made or is likely to make donations to the university (sometimes because they are alumni of the college themselves). And of course, some take race into consideration as part of that holistic process.

Beyond race, each of the other factors can also seem problematic to some, for multiple reasons. Take the SAT. Advocates for the SAT argue that its role as a common measure of academic achievement is useful in conjunction with other considerations.[4] Critics point out that the SAT is highly correlated with race and household income, and high school grades are better predictors of college grades than a student's SAT score.[5] Indeed, the increasingly common decision (particularly at larger, less selective private colleges) of not requiring SAT scores has led to a modest increase in admitted students who are Black, Latinx, or working class.[6] Still, eliminating the SAT is not enough to achieve racial equity; it depends on what takes its place. One study showed that the content of application essays, too, are correlated with household income, sometimes even more than SAT scores.[7] And not all types of colleges see an impact—for example, small liberal arts colleges that have gone SAT-optional have not always increased diversity in their student bodies as a result.[8] Other considerations, too, have a range of implications for equity.

Given the complexity of all the factors colleges consider, and the inequities baked into many of them, there is no perfect constellation of considerations for admission. In fact, each factor has winners and losers. Some produce more unequal outcomes than others, while some factors are dependent on particular talents or proclivities of students. They cater to different goals of universities, too. In other words, college admissions will never be completely "fair," and will never be objective. Indeed, this is an impossible task. Instead, we should view college admissions as an imperfect system, in which each university must make decisions in a world of unequal opportunities, with imperfect information about what students' future trajectories will be, and considering their own multiple purposes. It is certainly not a system of reward for individual achievement.

So, what should colleges do? Below I provide five recommendations for college admissions to better meet the goals of most colleges: teaching, research, contributions to society, and promoting equal opportunity. As we'll see, not all of them are explicitly tied to affirmative action. However, I include a broader set of recommendations given our discussion of bringing college admissions in line with university goals.

Expand affirmative action

First, given all the benefits to university missions highlighted throughout this book, selective colleges should expand their consideration of race in admissions. The legal attacks on affirmative action may require university legal teams to go beyond the diversity rationale of affirmative action in their arguments, and to consider how they might successfully defend affirmative action through an emphasis on equity, reparations, and social contributions. Even if the diversity argument is upheld in the latest US Supreme Court case, universities should find ways to incorporate the language of equity, reparations, and social contributions into talk about affirmative action. One way to do this is a clearer articulation of university goals, and how the admissions process fits into them. In doing so, universities should explicitly move away from language about selecting the "best," most worthy candidates, and move toward language discussing selecting candidates that further university objectives. That language should acknowledge how university needs and mission, along with chance and privilege, shape admissions decisions. This would be more honest, and would help shift mainstream discussions around college admissions toward a more realistic understanding of the process of selection.

Expand enrollment

Expanding enrollment would provide more opportunities for students to attend selective colleges.[9] The possibility of expansion reminds us that admissions is not about admitting only a certain kind of student; after all, we know that there are many more students who could succeed on elite college campuses than seats at those colleges currently (Harvard's president once said the university could fill each incoming class twice with valedictorians alone).[10] Indeed, there are historical precedents for the expansion of education to increase opportunities. In the nineteenth century, the Common Schools movement expanded free public education at the elementary level, and during the mid-twentieth century higher education rapidly grew, making it accessible to a broader range of Americans, regardless of their class backgrounds. Still, no movement to date has led to the expansion of elite higher education; instead, less selective and open-enrollment institutions have dramatically increased their enrollments.[11] Economists Peter Blair and Kent Smetters suggest that the trends in expansion at colleges with different admit rates (and lack thereof) show the high importance elite colleges seem to place on maintaining their status, an anti-inclusive instinct that flies in the face of increasing opportunities and contributing to the common good.[12] If enrollment expanded with the explicit aim of increasing racial diversity, the need for affirmative action would be attenuated (but not eliminated altogether).

Greater contextualization

One thing many, if not most, Americans interested in college admissions will agree on is that an applicant's accomplishments should be considered in the context of the opportunities they have had. This could mean, for example, admitting students with lower standardized test scores or fewer honors classes than others who attended different schools, as long as they outperformed peers at their own schools at a higher rate.

Contextualizing a student's achievements recognizes the undeniably unequal opportunities available to children in the United States and assuages the very real concern that those unequal opportunities rig the admissions process.

While contextualization may be obvious, not everyone believes in it. For example, in research for my book *The Diversity Bargain*, I found that most US students expressed support for contextualization, but most British students did not. One Oxford student told me, "I think Oxford strives for excellence, and I think they should always choose a brilliant candidate before looking at where he's from, or what color he is." Another told me she believes that in admissions, "ultimately we should all just be blank faces; we should all just be admitted totally on merit." Still, in recent years British universities have been pushed by government regulators to contextualize applicants, often by noting whether they live in disadvantaged neighborhoods that haven't sent students to elite universities, whether they attend low-performing schools, or whether they have spent time in foster care.[13] Even the US College Board, which has administered the SAT for nearly a century, jumped on board in 2019 by crafting an "adversity" score for test-takers. (Critics challenged the adversity score for, among other things, reducing complex life circumstances to a single number, and for using language that suggests deficits in those who experience hardship; the College Board quickly abandoned the adversity score after a public outcry).[14]

To better contextualize applicants, colleges should put more emphasis than they already do on the high schools students attend, the neighborhoods in which they live, and the education, income, and wealth levels of their parent(s) when considering opportunities.

But what about race?

One way to account for racial differences in opportunities is to implement a top percentage plan. University of Texas (UT) did this two decades ago after the 1996 *Hopwood v. Texas* US Court of Appeals decision, which barred race-conscious admissions. Under the plan, Texas students graduating in the top 10 percent of their high school class were automatically admitted to any UT campus. Because of the segregation of Texas high schools, this enabled more Black and Latinx students to attend the state's flagship school, UT Austin, than would have been admitted otherwise.

What were the outcomes of this policy? On the one hand, it was successful in identifying high achievers across the state of Texas, many of whom came from high schools from which very few, if any, students historically attended UT Austin.[15] In addition, students admitted under the program were more likely to graduate than if they had attended lower-tier colleges.[16] On the other hand, the policy was not able to restore the percentages of Black and Latinx students on the UT Austin campus that existed under affirmative action.[17] Some privileged students also changed their behaviors, attending lower-ranked high schools than they would have otherwise, to make it into the top 10 percent; this had a small but significant impact on the number of underrepresented minorities accepted under the plan.[18] Thus, this kind of percentage-based policy seems like an important way to increase geographic diversity, but cannot substitute for race-based affirmative action.

Even with greater consideration of class- and neighborhood-related factors such as those described above, contextualization requires paying attention to race. As I have described in this book, race matters for the achievements of children. When we recognize how race continues to shape opportunities in the United States, we can see how inequality today is, at least in part, due to the lingering effects of racial exclusion from the past. And then, it is hard *not* to advocate for seeing race as another important contextualizing factor. We simply don't have better measures of all the privileges and disadvantages shaped by race in the United States.

And affirmative action does not need to compete with the consideration of class in admissions. This is not an either-or proposition.

Make ability to pay less significant

Spending on US higher education is regressive. The best prepared, most privileged students tend to attend universities with the most resources, while students with the weakest preparation and fewest economic resources tend to attend the least resourced colleges. This is also true with respect to race—Black and Latinx college students are more likely to attend lower-status colleges, which have the fewest resources, while white and Asian American students are more likely than Black and Latinx students to attend the most selective colleges.[19] In the past, many states explicitly provided sub-par college opportunities to Black students compared to white students.[20] At the same time, college costs and student loans have skyrocketed. Given declining state aid to higher education, the costs even for students attending in-state public universities and two-year colleges have more than doubled in the past three decades.[21] The complexities of getting financial aid and the actual (rather than the publicly disclosed) cost of college also remain barriers for low-income students.[22]

The federal government has helped to (partially) correct the pattern of unequal education at the K12 level, by providing significant funding to schools and districts serving large numbers of low-income children, providing breakfast and lunch to low-income children at school, and more. Now that college is more critical than ever, the federal government should play a similar role in higher education. Pell Grant awards should be expanded, and for-profit colleges should be scrutinized for their added value for potential students.[23] The federal government should provide considerably more aid to colleges that educate student bodies that are majority first-generation, working class, and underrepresented minority. States, too, should shore up their funding for state colleges, given those colleges' roles as engines of social mobility.[24] In recent decades, just as underrepresented minorities began to attend state colleges in larger and larger numbers, states began dramatically cutting funding to those colleges.[25]

The federal government as well as state governments should also rethink the benefits currently provided to universities with large endowments, since they aid a student body that is already mostly well-off. President Trump first raised this issue, instituting a so-called "endowment tax" of 1.4% on the investment income earned by universities that hold more than half a million dollars in assets per student.[26] This affects about four dozen of the thousands of colleges in the country.[27] New legislation should ensure that those taxes go toward support for colleges that promote social mobility, including effective community colleges.[28] State governments and the federal government could also tie tax-exempt status to guidelines about what percentage of students come from lower-income families, and a college's role in promoting social mobility. Britain has had some success with this model. There, public universities must create "widening participation" agreements with the government that describe how they will increase access to their universities.[29]

The above changes will go a long way to ensuring that promising applicants will have the opportunity to study at a selective college. For their part, colleges should consider boosting their financial aid budgets and finding ways to reduce spending—for example, through reducing the growing number of administrative positions, reconsidering expenses on increasingly lavish student centers, and more. Given the history of racial exclusion on elite college campuses and the impact of racial exclusion on economic means, increasing funding in various ways would have a direct impact on the number of underrepresented minorities on selective college campuses. Such shifts would be important complements to affirmative action. And they would ensure that the student bodies on selective college campuses are more representative of young adults in the United States today.

An admissions lottery

Any way that students are selected to study at elite colleges, there are winners and losers. Because there are multiple purposes and goals on any given selective college campus—let alone across college campuses or among ordinary Americans—finding consensus on how to admit students is almost impossible. We don't agree on what we're looking for, and even if we agreed, we have imperfect information when trying to select students based on those criteria. And measuring opportunity is also impossible to do with precision. However, we present admissions as a process that selects the "best," "most deserving" applicants, which can make the people who don't directly benefit from affirmative action less willing to support it. That is, because they feel they earned their spot at the elite college fairly (which ignores the privileges they had that helped them achieve excellence), they feel justified when greater benefits accrue to them—better jobs, social connections, and more that come with attending an elite university. And they can feel that beneficiaries of affirmative action did not similarly earn their place at the table.

An admissions lottery would change that. We would no longer be able to say that the winners in society deserve their fortunes, just as those at the bottom of the pile supposedly deserve theirs. A lottery would make it clear that luck plays a role in college admissions, and that there are many young people who are just as worthy as those admitted, but who were not as lucky. Previous studies have shown that increasing selectivity has led to increased emphasis on SAT scores to parse out students, with implications for racial inequality, especially absent affirmative action.[30] This means that entering students into a lottery based on an SAT score cutoff, rather than admitting top students by SAT score, would reduce the need for affirmative action to compensate for racial inequality in SAT scores.[31]

Lottery eligibility could require a specific level of demonstrated academic skill. In addition, a lottery could give different "weights"—more tickets that increase your chances of being selected—for other qualities, such as sports skills or being part of an under-represented group on campus. Evaluation of applicants' eligibility for a lottery could even be holistic.

An admissions lottery would be a more honest system, and one in which, I believe, there would be more support for affirmative action. It would go a long way toward making admissions more equitable, reducing (but not eliminating) the need for affirmative action. No doubt, families of high achievers would protest an admissions lottery.[32] However, that opposition should not stop reforms designed to upend their hold on selective college education.

Beyond Admissions

Since the killing of George Floyd in 2020 greater attention has been paid to racial justice across our country—not just by individuals, but by corporations and colleges, too. This promising development suggests that when there is political will, even conservative, predominantly white organizations can make sincere efforts toward racial justice. I am hopeful that this momentum will continue. Affirmative action and other aspects of college admissions are just one mechanism to achieve the goals of equal opportunity, reparations, diverse classroom perspectives, and bettering our shared world. Other programs and policies can expand the number of underrepresented minority students admitted to selective college campuses, even absent changes to current admissions practices.

Providing more equitable educational opportunities earlier in life will go a long way toward reducing the need for affirmative action, because it aims, in part, to correct for the racially unequal outcomes that American K12 education produces. While many say this is the only way to address racial inequality in who goes to selective colleges, that solution ignores children going to school and applying to college in the coming years. So a dual commitment to increasing equity in K12 education alongside affirmative action is the way forward.

Second, families and employers should put less stake in college admissions. When we recognize the diverse goals that universities attempt to address through college admissions, it becomes clear that admission is not a certification of individual merit or deservingness, nor was it ever meant to be. Students and parents would do well to heed *New York Times* columnist Frank Bruni's message in the title of his book, *Where You Go Is Not Who You'll Be.* And employers should look well beyond the few selective colleges they prefer when recruiting the next generation of professionals, as well.

Finally, rather than subscribe wholeheartedly to what Grubb and Lazerson call the "education gospel," we should double down on support for working-class people in the United States. Two-thirds of American adults do not hold a bachelor's degree. And most of those who do go to college never attend a selective college. These adults, too, deserve a decent standard of living, which will be made possible not by tweaks to admissions, but rather by raising the minimum wage, supporting unions, expanding health care access and housing support, and promoting well-paying jobs for low-skilled workers. These supports are critical for the well-being of all Americans, whether or not they ever step onto a college campus.

Affirmative action has long been a flashpoint, because it is a clear manifestation of a topic we don't like to discuss: how we should move beyond our history of racism and racial exclusion. As our political divide becomes increasingly polarized, so too do entrenched views on affirmative action. Political polarization makes it hard to clearly see the complexity of a policy that has been servant to many masters, and now hangs from a thin legal thread. If we are to truly transform racial inequality in the United States, we cannot rely on this one precarious mechanism. Real racial equity requires so much more, and a commitment to pursuing equity no matter what our political identities or university preferences. We must go well beyond this single precarious policy to make the American dream a reality.

I found myself compelled to write this book for two reasons. The first was a belief that I had something important to add to a public conversation that involves increasing attacks on affirmative action. The second, and probably more important to getting the ideas on the page was the gentle but persistent encouragement from Jonathan Skerrett at Polity Press that I do so. As much as I resisted his reminders, I am grateful for Jonathan's nudges to get it done. Jonathan, Irene Browne, Peter Levine, Helen Marrow, and Yami Rodriguez all provided feedback on a draft of the manuscript. So did Ellen Berrey, Stephen Steinberg, and another anonymous reviewer for Polity Press. David Lobenstine helped me strengthen the prose. Sophia Costa, Shelby Austin-Manning, Ann Klefstad, and others at Polity copy-edited, proofread, and indexed meticulously. Countless others have shaped my thinking on affirmative action in our conversations—Margaret Chin, Nadirah Farah Foley, OiYan Poon, Janelle Wong, and Michaele Turnage Young, to name a few. I'm grateful to conversations with the late Lani Guinier many years ago that were important for my thinking on this topic, as well. My colleagues at Tufts sociology have created a culture that enabled me to get this book done despite so much else happening on our campus and in the world around us. As always, my biggest gratitude is for my family—Ramesh, Zoya, Kavi, Nuria, my parents, my brother, the Kumar family, and the best aunts, uncles, and cousins, too—and friends far and near, many of whom know nothing of this book but mean the world to me. They all keep me going, and more important, they provide the absolute best distractions from the arduous writing process.

Aisch, G. L. Buchanan, A. Cox, and K. Quealy. 2017. "Some Colleges Have More Students From the Top 1 Percent Than the Bottom 60. Find Yours." *The New York Times.* Accessed October 24, 2021. https://www.nytimes.com/interactive/2017/01/18/upshot /some-colleges-have-more-students-from-the-top-1-percent-than -the-bottom-60.html

Alba, R. D. 2020. *The Great Demographic Illusion: Majority, Minority, and the Expanding American Mainstream.* Princeton, NJ: Princeton University Press.

Alba, R. D., J. R. Logan, and B. J. Stults. 2000. "How Segregated Are Middle-Class African Americans?" *Social Problems* 47(4): 543–558.

Alon, S., and M. Tienda. 2005. "Assessing the 'Mismatch' Hypothesis: Differences in College Graduation Rates by Institutional Selectivity." *Sociology of Education* 78(4): 294–315.

Alon, S., and M. Tienda. 2007. "Diversity, Opportunity, and the Shifting Meritocracy in Higher Education." *American Sociological Review* 72(4): 487–511.

Alvero, A., S. Giebel, B. Gebre-Medhin, A. L. Antonio, M. L. Stevens, and B. W. Domingue. 2021. "Essay Content and Style are Strongly Related to Household Income and SAT Scores: Evidence from 60,000 Undergraduate Applications." *Science Advances* 7(42).

Anderson, N. 2021. "Applications Boom, Admit Rates Plummet: Prestige College Admissions Get a Little Crazier in the Pandemic."

References

Washington Post. Accessed December 15, 2021. https://www.washingtonpost.com/education/2021/04/07/admit-rates-ivy-league-pandemic-test-optional/

Antonio, A. L. 2001. "Diversity and the Influence of Friendship Groups in College." *Review of Higher Education: Journal of the Association for the Study of Higher Education* 25(1): 63–89.

Arcidiacono, P., E. M. Aucejo, and V. J. Hotz. 2016. "University Differences in the Graduation of Minorities in STEM Fields: Evidence from California." *American Economic Review* 106(3): 525–562.

Avery, C., C. Hoxby, C. Jackson, K. Burek, G. Pope, and M. Raman. 2006. "Cost Should Be No Barrier: An Evaluation of the First Year of Harvard's Financial Aid Initiative." *National Bureau of Economic Research Working Paper Series.* Accessed April 1, 2022. https://www.nber.org/papers/w12029

Baker, D. J., and M. N. Bastedo. 2022. "What If We Leave It Up to Chance? Admissions Lotteries and Equitable Access at Selective Colleges." *Educational Researcher* 51(2): 98–108.

Ballotpedia. n.d. "Affirmative Action on the Ballot." Accessed March 29, 2022. https://ballotpedia.org/Affirmative_action_on_the_ballot

Barnes, R. 2014. "Justice Sonia Sotomayor Defends Affirmative Action." *Washington Post.* Accessed October 15, 2021. https://www.washingtonpost.com/national/justice-sonia-sotomayor-defends-affirmative-action/2014/06/22/cfdbe774-fa22-11e3-8176-f2c941cf35f1_story.html

Batalova, J., M. Hanna, and C. Levesque. 2021. "Frequently Requested Statistics on Immigrants and Immigration in the United States." *Migration Policy Institute.* Accessed March 3, 2021. https://www.migrationpolicy.org/article/frequently-requested-statistics-immigrants-and-immigration-united-states-2020#demographic-educational-linguistic

References

Belasco, A. S., K. O. Rosinger, and J. C. Hearn. 2015. "The Test-Optional Movement at America's Selective Liberal Arts Colleges: A Boon for Equity or Something Else?" *Educational Evaluation and Policy Analysis* 37(2): 206–223.

Bell, D. 1979. "Brown v. Board of Education and the Interest-Convergence Dilemma." *Harvard Law Review* 93: 518–533.

Bellah, R. N. 1985. *Habits of the Heart: Individualism and Commitment in American Life*. Berkeley: University of California Press.

Bennett, C. T. 2022. "Untested Admissions: Examining Changes in Application Behaviors and Student Demographics Under Test-Optional Policies." *American Educational Research Journal* 59(1): 180–216.

Berrey, E. 2015. *The Enigma of Diversity: The Language of Race and the Limits of Racial Justice*. Chicago, IL: University of Chicago Press.

Berrey, E. C. 2011. "Why Diversity Became Orthodox in Higher Education, and How It Changed the Meaning of Race on Campus." *Critical Sociology* 37(5): 573–596.

Black, S. F., J. T. Denning, and J. Rothstein. 2020. "Winners and Losers? The Effect of Gaining and Losing Access to Selective Colleges on Education and Labor Market Outcomes." *National Bureau of Economic Research Working Paper Series*. Accessed April 1, 2022. https://www.nber.org/papers/26821

Blair, P. Q., and K. Smetters. 2021. "Why Don't Elite Colleges Expand Supply?" *National Bureau of Economic Research Working Paper Series*. Accessed April 1, 2022. https://www.nber.org/papers/29309

Bleemer, Z. 2020. "Mismatch at the University of California before Proposition 209." *UC-CHP Policy Brief 2020.5* Accessed March 31, 2021. https://zacharybleemer.com/wp-content/uploads/Policy-Briefs/UC-CHP-2020.5-Mismatch.pdf

Bleemer, Z. 2021. "Affirmative Action, Mismatch and Economic Mobility After California's Proposition 209." *Quarterly Journal of Economics* 137(1): 115–160.

Bobo, L. 1998. "Race, Interests, and Beliefs About Affirmative Action: Unanswered Questions and New Directions." *American Behavioral Scientist* 41(7): 985–1003.

Bobo, L., and J. R. Kluegel. 1993. "Opposition to Race-Targeting: Self-interest, Stratification Ideology, or Racial Attitudes?" *American Sociological Review* 58(4): 443–464.

Bonilla-Silva, E. 2003. *Racism without Racists: Color-Blind Racism and the Persistence of Racial Inequality in the United States.* Lanham, MD: Rowman & Littlefield.

Bosman, J. 2021. "Chicago Suburb Shapes Reparations for Black Residents: 'It Is the Start'." *The New York Times.* Accessed October 17, 2021. https://www.nytimes.com/2021/03/22/us/reparations-evanston-illinois-housing.html

Bowen, W. G., and D. C. Bok. 1998. *The Shape of the River: Long-term Consequences of Considering Race in College and University Admissions.* Princeton, NJ: Princeton University Press.

Bowen, W. G., and S. A. Levin. 2003. *Reclaiming the Game: College Sports and Educational Values.* Princeton, NJ: Princeton University Press.

Bowman, N. A. 2010. "College Diversity Experiences and Cognitive Development: A Meta-Analysis." *Review of Educational Research* 80(1): 4–33.

Bowman, N. A. 2011. "Promoting Participation in a Diverse Democracy: A Meta-Analysis of College Diversity Experiences and Civic Engagement." *Review of Educational Research* 81(1): 29–68.

Brint, S. 2019. *Two Cheers for Higher Education: Why American Universities Are Stronger Than Ever—and How to Meet the Challenges They Face.* Princeton, NJ: Princeton University Press.

Brint, S. G., and J. Karabel. 1989. *The Diverted Dream: Community Colleges and the Promise of Educational Opportunity in America, 1900-1985.* New York: Oxford University Press.

References

Brown University Steering Committee on Slavery and Justice. n.d. "Slavery and Justice: Report of the Brown University Steering Committee on Slavery and Justice." Accessed December 15, 2021. https://cssj.brown.edu/sites/g/files/dprerj861/files/pdfs/CSSJ%20Report%20(Corrected)_0.pdf

Carey, J., K. Clayton, and Y. Horiuchi. 2019. *Campus Diversity: The Hidden Consensus.* Cambridge, UK: Cambridge University Press.

Carnevale, A. P., and J. Strohl. 2013. "Separate and Unequal: How Higher Education Reform Reinforces the Intergenerational Reproduction of White Racial Privilege." Accessed April 2, 2015. https://1gyhoq479ufd3yna29x7ubjn-wpengine.netdna-ssl.com/wp-content/uploads/SeparateUnequal.FR_.pdf

Carney, J. 1995. "Affirmative Action: Mend It, Don't End It." *Time.* Accessed October 15, 2021. http://content.time.com/time/subscriber/article/0,33009,983257,00.html

Carson, J. 2003. "The Culture of Intelligence." In *The Cambridge History of Science.* Eds. T. M. Porter and D. Ross. Cambridge, UK: Cambridge University Press.

Cashin, S. 2015. *Place, Not Race: A New Vision of Opportunity in America.* Boston: Beacon Press.

Chang, M. J. 1999. "Does Racial Diversity Matter? The Educational Impact of a Racially Diverse Undergraduate Population." *Journal of College Student Development* 40(4): 377–395.

Cheryan, S., and B. Monin. 2005. "Where Are You 'Really' From?: Asian Americans and Identity Denial." *Journal of Personality and Social Psychology* 89(5): 717–730.

Chin, M. J., D. M. Quinn, T. K. Dhaliwal, and V. S. Lovison. 2020. "Bias in the Air: A Nationwide Exploration of Teachers' Implicit Racial Attitudes, Aggregate Bias, and Student Outcomes." *Educational Researcher* 49(8): 566–578.

Chin, M. M. 2020. *Stuck: Why Asian Americans Don't Reach the Top of the Corporate Ladder.* New York: New York University Press.

References

Choi, A., K. Herbert, and O. Winslow. 2019. "Long Island Divided." *New York Newsday*. Accessed March 4, 2021. https://projects.newsday.com/long-island/real-estate-agents-investigation/

Coates, T.-N. 2014. "The Case for Reparations." *The Atlantic*. Accessed July 8, 2014. http://www.theatlantic.com/features/archive/2014/05/the-case-for-reparations/361631/

Cortes, K. E. 2010. "Do Bans on Affirmative Action Hurt Minority Students? Evidence from the Texas Top 10% Plan." *Economics of Education Review* 29(6): 1110–1124.

Cortes, K. E., and D. Klasik. 2021. "Uniform Admissions, Unequal Access: Did the Top 10% Plan Increase Access to Selective Flagship Institutions?" *IZA Discussion Paper*. Accessed October 24, 2021. https://papers.ssrn.com/sol3/papers.cfm?abstract_id=3758689

Counsel for President and Fellows of Harvard College. 2018. "Memorandum in support of defendant's motion for summary judgment on all remaining counts." Accessed March 29, 2022. https://projects.iq.harvard.edu/files/diverse-education/files/harvardsummaryjudgment

Cullen, J. B., M. C. Long, and R. Reback. 2013. "Jockeying for Position: Strategic High School Choice under Texas' Top Ten Percent Plan." *Journal of Public Economics* 97: 32–48.

Dale, S. B., and A. B. Krueger. 2002. "Estimating the Payoff to Attending a More Selective College: An Application of Selection on Observables and Unobservables." *The Quarterly Journal of Economics* 117(4): 1491–1527.

Dale, S. B., and A. B. Krueger. 2011. "Estimating the Return to College Selectivity over the Career Using Administrative Earnings Data." *National Bureau of Economic Research Working Paper Series*. Accessed April 3, 2015. http://www.nber.org/papers/w17159.pdf

Darity, W. A. 2020. *From Here to Equality: Reparations for Black Americans in the Twenty-First Century*. Chapel Hill: The University of North Carolina Press.

References

Daugherty, L., I. McFarlin, and P. Martorell. 2014. "The Texas Ten Percent Plan's Impact on College Enrollment." *Education Next.* Accessed October 24, 2021. https://www.educationnext.org/texas -ten-percent-plans-impact-college-enrollment/

Davern, M. R. Bautista, J. Freese, S. L. Morgan, and T. W. Smith. General Social Surveys, 1972–2021. Sponsored by National Science Foundation. Chicago: NORC, 2021: NORC at the University of Chicago. Data accessed from the GSS Data Explorer website at gssdataexplorer.norc.org

Dee, T. S. 2004. "Teachers, Race and Student Achievement in a Randomized Experiment." *The Review of Economics and Statistics* 86 (1): 195–210.

Diaz, J. 2020. "This Florida Student Was Accepted at All 8 Ivy League Schools. (He Chose Yale.)." *The New York Times.* Accessed December 15, 2021. https://www.nytimes.com/2020/04/26/us /craig-mcfarland-ivy-league-accepted.html

Dow, D. M. 2019. *Mothering While Black: Boundaries and Burdens of Middle-Class Parenthood.* Oakland: University of California Press.

Duru-Bellat, M., and E. Tenret. 2012. "Who's for Meritocracy? Individual and Contextual Variations in the Faith." *Comparative Education Review* 56(2): 223–247.

Dworkin, R. 1977. "Why Bakke Has No Case." *The New York Review of Books.* Accessed December 16, 2021. https://www.nybooks.com /articles/1977/11/10/why-bakke-has-no-case/

Dworkin, R. 2012. "The Case Against Color-Blind Admissions." *The New York Review of Books.* Accessed December 16, 2021. https:// www.nybooks.com/articles/2012/12/20/case-against-color-blind -admissions/

Dynarski, S., C. J. Libassi, K. Michelmore, and S. Owen. 2020. "Closing the Gap: The Effect of a Targeted, Tuition-Free Promise on College Choices of High-Achieving, Low-Income Students."

References

National Bureau of Economic Research Working Paper Series. Accessed April 1, 2022. https://www.nber.org/papers/25349

Epps, G. 2014. "On Race and Voter ID, John Roberts Wants It Both Ways." *The Atlantic.* Accessed October 15, 2021. https://www.theatlantic.com/politics/archive/2014/10/on-race-and-voter-id-john-roberts-wants-it-both-ways/381868/

Espeland, W. N., and M. Sauder. 2007. "Rankings and Reactivity: How Public Measures Recreate Social Worlds." *American Journal of Sociology* 113(1): 1–40.

Espeland, W. N., and M. Sauder. 2016. *Engines of Anxiety: Academic Rankings, Reputation, and Accountability.* New York: Russell Sage Foundation.

Espinosa, L. L., J. M. Turk, M. Taylor, and H. M. Chessman. 2019. "Race and Ethnicity in Higher Education: A Status Report." *American Council on Education.* Accessed May 24, 2022. https://1xfsu31b52d33idlp13twtos-wpengine.netdna-ssl.com/wp-content/uploads/2019/02/Race-and-Ethnicity-in-Higher-Education.pdf

Esterline, C., and J. Batalova. 2022. "Frequently Requested Statistics on Immigrants and Immigration in the United States." *Migration Policy Institute.* Accessed April 1, 2022. https://www.migrationpolicy.org/article/frequently-requested-statistics-immigrants-and-immigration-united-states#unauthorized

Fandos, N. 2021. "House Panel Advances Bill to Study Reparations in Historic Vote." *The New York Times.* Accessed October 16, 2021. https://www.nytimes.com/2021/04/14/us/politics/reparations-slavery-house.html

Fischer, M. J. 2008. "Does Campus Diversity Promote Friendship Diversity? A Look at Interracial Friendships in College." *Social Science Quarterly* 89(3): 631–655.

Fisher v. University of Texas at Austin. 2013. 570 U.S. 297.

Fisher v. University of Texas at Austin. 2016. 579 U.S.

References

Fishman, S. H. 2020. "Educational Mobility among the Children of Asian American Immigrants." *American Journal of Sociology* 126(2): 260–317.

Fiske, S. T., J. Xu, A. C. Cuddy, and P. Glick. 1999. "(Dis)respecting versus (Dis)liking: Status and Interdependence Predict Ambivalent Stereotypes of Competence and Warmth." *Journal of Social Issues* 55(3): 473–489.

Gallup. 2018. "Americans' Views on Affirmative Action Programs for Women and Minorities (Trends)." *Gallup News Service.* Accessed October 15, 2021. https://news.gallup.com/poll/247130 /americans-views-affirmative-action-programs-women-minorities -trends.aspx

Gartsbeyn, M. 2021. "Harvard Announces Lowest Ever Acceptance Rate After Surge in Applications." *Boston.com.* Accessed October 15, 2021. https://www.boston.com/news/education/2021/04/07 /harvard-low-acceptance-rate/

Geismer, L. 2015. *Don't Blame Us: Suburban Liberals and the Transformation of the Democratic Party.* Princeton, NJ: Princeton University Press.

Graham, D. 2014. "How to Get Into Harvard." *The Atlantic.* Accessed April 1, 2022. https://www.theatlantic.com/education /archive/2014/06/how-to-get-into-harvard/373726/

Gratz v. Bollinger. 2003. 539 U.S. 244.

Grofman, B., and S. Merrill. 2004. "Anticipating Likely Consequences of Lottery-Based Affirmative Action." *Social Science Quarterly* 85(5): 1447–1468.

Grutter v. Bollinger. 2003. 539 U.S. 306.

Guinier, L. 2001. "Colleges Should Take 'Confirmative Action' in Admissions." *Chronicle of Higher Education.* Accessed July 3, 2014. http://chronicle.com/article/Colleges-Should-Take/22060/

Guinier, L. 2015. *The Tyranny of the Meritocracy: Democratizing Higher Education in America.* Boston: Beacon Press.

References

Gurin, P. 1999. "Expert Report of Patricia Gurin." *Michigan Journal of Race & Law* 5(1): 363–425.

Gurin, P., E. L. Dey, S. Hurtado, and G. Gurin. 2002. "Diversity and Higher Education: Theory and Impact on Educational Outcomes." *Harvard Educational Review* 72(3): 330.

Hagerman, M. A. 2018. *White Kids: Growing Up with Privilege in a Racially Divided America*. New York: New York University Press.

Hamilton, L. T., and K. Nielsen. 2021. *Broke: The Racial Consequences of Underfunding Public Universities.* Chicago, IL: University of Chicago Press.

Harris, A. 2021. *The State Must Provide: Why America's Colleges Have Always Been Unequal—and How to Set Them Right.* New York: Ecco.

Harris, A. L. 2011. *Kids Don't Want to Fail: Oppositional Culture and Black Students' Academic Achievement*. Cambridge, MA: Harvard University Press.

Hartocollis, A. 2019. "SAT 'Adversity Score' Is Abandoned in Wake of Criticism." *The New York Times*. Accessed October 22, 2021. https://www.nytimes.com/2019/08/27/us/sat-adversity-score-college-board.html

Harvard Gazette, The. 2011. "An unprecedented admissions year." Accessed October 15, 2021. https://news.harvard.edu/gazette/story/2011/03/an-unprecedented-admissions-year/

Hextrum, K. 2018. "The Hidden Curriculum of College Athletic Recruitment." *Harvard Educational Review* 88(3): 355–377.

Hirschman, D., and E. Berrey. 2017. "The Partial Deinstitutionalization of Affirmative Action in U.S. Higher Education, 1988–2014." *Sociological Science* 4: 449–468.

Hook, J. V. 2019. "Profile of the Unauthorized Population: United States." *Migration Policy Institute*. Accessed December 16, 2021. https://www.migrationpolicy.org/data/unauthorized-immigrant-population/state/US

References

Hoxby, C. M., and C. Avery. 2012. The Missing "One-Offs": The Hidden Supply of High-Achieving, Low Income Students." *National Bureau of Economic Research Working Paper Series*. Accessed April 1, 2022. https://www.nber.org/papers/w18586

Hsin, A., and Y. Xie. 2014. "Explaining Asian Americans' Academic Advantage over Whites." *Proceedings of the National Academy of Sciences* 111(23): 8416–8421.

Hsu, H. 2018. "The Rise and Fall of Affirmative Action." *The New Yorker*. Accessed October 15, 2021. https://www.newyorker.com/magazine/2018/10/15/the-rise-and-fall-of-affirmative-action

Huang, T. J. 2021. "Negotiating the Workplace: Second-generation Asian American Professionals' Early Experiences." *Journal of Ethnic and Migration Studies* 47(11): 2477–2496.

Huerto, R., and E. Lindo. 2020. "Minority Patients Benefit from Having Minority Doctors, but That's a Hard Match to Make." *The Conversation*. Accessed March 29, 2022. https://theconversation.com/minority-patients-benefit-from-having-minority-doctors-but-thats-a-hard-match-to-make-130504

Hutchings, V. L., and N. A. Valentino. 2004. "The Centrality of Race in American Politics." *Annual Review of Political Science* 7(1): 383–408.

Iceland, J., and R. Wilkes. 2014. "Does Socioeconomic Status Matter? Race, Class, and Residential Segregation." *Social Problems* 53(2): 248–273.

Jacoby-Senghor, D., S. Sinclair, and J. N. Shelton. 2016. "A Lesson in Bias: The Relationship Between Implicit Racial Bias and Performance in Pedagogical Contexts." *Journal of Experimental Social Psychology* 63: 50–55.

Jayakumar, U. M. 2008. "Can Higher Education Meet the Needs of an Increasingly Diverse and Global Society? Campus Diversity and Cross-Cultural Workforce Competencies." *Harvard Educational Review* 78(4): 615–651.

References

Jayakumar, U. M., and S. E. Page. 2021. "Cultural Capital and Opportunities for Exceptionalism: Bias in University Admissions." *The Journal of Higher Education* 92(7): 1109–1139.

Johnson, H. B. 2006. *The American Dream and the Power of Wealth: Choosing Schools and Inheriting Inequality in the Land of Opportunity*. New York: Routledge.

Johnson, L. B. 1965. Commencement Address at Howard University: "To Fulfill These Rights." The American Presidency Project. Accessed October 15, 2021. https://www.presidency.ucsb.edu/documents/commencement-address-howard-university-fulfill-these-rights

Kahlenberg, R. D. 1996. *The Remedy: Class, Race, and Affirmative Action*. New York: BasicBooks.

Karabel, J. 2005. *The Chosen: The Hidden History of Admission and Exclusion at Harvard, Yale, and Princeton*. Boston, MA: Houghton Mifflin.

Katznelson, I. 2005. *When Affirmative Action Was White: An Untold History of Racial Inequality in Twentieth-Century America*. New York: W.W. Norton.

Kaushal, N., K. Magnuson, and J. Waldfogel. 2011. "How Is Family Income Related to Investments in Children's Learning?" In *Whither Opportunity? Rising Inequality, Schools, and Children's Life Chances*. Ed. G. J. Duncan and R. J. Murnane. New York: Russell Sage Foundation.

Kehal, P. S., D. Hirschman, and E. Berrey. 2021. "When Affirmative Action Disappears: Unexpected Patterns in Student Enrollments at Selective U.S. Institutions, 1990–2016." *Sociology of Race and Ethnicity* 7(4): 543–560.

Kerr, C. 2001. *The Uses of the University* (5th ed.). Cambridge, MA: Harvard University Press.

Kidder, W. 2013. "A High Target for 'Mismatch': Bogus Arguments about Affirmative Action." *Los Angeles Review of Books*. Accessed

October 17, 2021. https://lareviewofbooks.org/article/a-high-target-for-mismatch-bogus-arguments-about-affirmative-action/

Kim, C. J. 1999. "The Racial Triangulation of Asian Americans." *Politics & Society* 27(1): 105–138.

Kirp, D. L. 2021. "Why Stanford Should Clone Itself." *The New York Times*. Accessed October 17, 2021. https://www.nytimes.com/2021/04/06/opinion/stanford-admissions-campus.html

Kochhar, R., and A. Cilluffo. 2018. "Key Findings on the Rise in Income Inequality within America's Racial and Ethnic Groups." *Pew Research Center*. Accessed October 17, 2021. https://www.pewresearch.org/fact-tank/2018/07/12/key-findings-on-the-rise-in-income-inequality-within-americas-racial-and-ethnic-groups/

Kohli, S. 2015. "Obama Wants Community College to be 'As Free and Universal' as High School." *Quartz*. Accessed October 15, 2021. https://qz.com/330264/obama-wants-community-college-to-be-as-free-and-universal-as-high-school/

Krogstad, J. M., and J. Radford. 2018. "Education Levels of U.S. Immigrants are on the Rise." Pew Research Center. Accessed May 23, 2022. https://www.pewresearch.org/fact-tank/2018/09/14/education-levels-of-u-s-immigrants-are-on-the-rise/

Laar, C. V., S. Levin, S. Sinclair, and J. Sidanius. 2005. "The Effect of University Roommate Contact on Ethnic Attitudes and Behavior." *Journal of Experimental Social Psychology* 41(4): 329–345.

Lacy, K. R. 2007. *Blue-chip Black: Race, Class, and Status in the New Black Middle Class*. Berkeley: University of California Press.

Laforce, T. 2018. "Why Do Asian-Americans Remain Largely Unseen in Film and Television?" *The New York Times*. Accessed October 17, 2021. https://www.nytimes.com/2018/11/06/t-magazine/asian-american-actors-representation.html

Lareau, A. 2011. *Unequal Childhoods: Class, Race, and Family Life*. Berkeley: University of California Press.

References

Lee, J., and M. Zhou. 2015. *The Asian American Achievement Paradox*. New York: Russell Sage Foundation.

Levin, B. 2021. "Anti-Asian Hate Crime Reported to Police in Large U.S. Cities: 2021 & 2020." *Center for the Study of Hate & Extremism, California State University, San Bernardino*. Accessed May 20, 2022. https://www.csusb.edu/sites/default/files/Report%20to%20 the%20Nation%20-%20Anti-Asian%20Hate%202020%20 Final%20Draft%20-%20As%20of%20Apr%2030%202021%20 6%20PM%20corrected.pdf

Lewis-McCoy, R. L. H. 2014. *Inequality in the Promised Land: Race, Resources, and Suburban Schooling*. Stanford, CA: Stanford University Press.

Lewis, A. E., and J. Diamond. 2015. *Despite the Best Intentions: How Racial Inequality Thrives in Good Schools*. New York: Oxford University Press.

Li, G., and L. Wang. 2008. *Model Minority Myth Revisited: An Interdisciplinary Approach to Demystifying Asian American Educational Experiences*. Charlotte, NC: Information Age Publishing.

Lin, M. H., V. S. Y. Kwan, A. Cheung, and S. T. Fiske. 2005. "Stereotype Content Model Explains Prejudice for an Envied Outgroup: Scale of Anti-Asian American Stereotypes." *Personality and Social Psychology Bulletin* 31(1): 34–47.

Lipset, S. M. 1975. *Education and Politics at Harvard: Two Essays Prepared for the Carnegie Commission on Higher Education*. New York: McGraw-Hill.

Liptak, A., and A. Hartocollis. 2022. "Supreme Court Will Hear Challenge to Affirmative Action at Harvard and U.N.C." *The New York Times*. Accessed May 23, 2022. https://www.nytimes.com /2022/01/24/us/politics/supreme-court-affirmative-action-harvard -unc.html

Long, M. C., and N. A. Bateman. 2020. "Long-Run Changes in Underrepresentation After Affirmative Action Bans in Public

Universities." *Educational Evaluation and Policy Analysis* 42(2): 188–207.

Long, M. C., V. Saenz, and M. Tienda. 2010. "Policy Transparency and College Enrollment: Did the Texas Top Ten Percent Law Broaden Access to the Public Flagships?" *The ANNALS of the American Academy of Political and Social Science* 627(1): 82–105.

Long, M. C., and M. Tienda. 2008. "Winners and Losers: Changes in Texas University Admissions Post-Hopwood." *Educational Evaluation and Policy Analysis* 30(3): 255–280.

Lu, V. E., and D. T. Tsotsong. 2021. "What Does Harvard's Record-Low Admissions Rate Mean For the College — And For Higher Education?" Accessed December 15, 2021. https://www.thecrimson.com/article/2021/4/30/low-acceptance-rate-implications/

Ma, J., M. Pender, and C. Libassi. 2020. "Trends in College Pricing and Student Aid 2020." *College Board.* Accessed March 24, 2022. https://research.collegeboard.org/media/pdf/trends-college-pricing-student-aid-2020.pdf

Massey, D. S., and N. A. Denton. 1993. *American Apartheid: Segregation and the Making of the Underclass.* Cambridge, MA: Harvard University Press.

Massey, D. S., M. Mooney, C. Z. Charles, and K. C. Torres. 2007. "Black Immigrants and Black Natives Attending Selective Colleges and Universities in the United States." *American Journal of Education* 113(2): 243.

McIntosh, K., E. Moss, R. Nunn, and J. Shambaugh. 2020. "Examining the Black-White Wealth Gap." *Brookings.* Accessed October 16, 2021. https://www.brookings.edu/blog/up-front/2020/02/27/examining-the-black-white-wealth-gap/

McKown, C., and R. S. Weinstein. 2008. "Teacher Expectations, Classroom Context, and the Achievement Gap." *Journal of School Psychology* 46(3): 235–261.

References

McMillan Cottom, T. 2016. "Georgetown's Slavery Announcement Is Remarkable. But It's Not Reparations." *Vox*. Accessed May 24, 2022. https://www.vox.com/2016/9/2/12773110/georgetown-slavery-admission-reparations

McMillan Cottom, T. 2017. *Lower Ed: The Troubling Rise of For-Profit Colleges in the New Economy Hardcover*. New York: The New Press.

Migration Policy Institute. 2019. "Educational Attainment of U.S. Adults (ages 25 and over) by Nativity and Select Country of Birth, 2019, (%)." Accessed March 24, 2022. https://www.migrationpolicy.org/sites/default/files/datahub/MPI-Data-Hub_EduAttainment-Nativity%20%26%20byCOB_2019.xlsx

Mijs, J. J. B. 2021. "The Paradox of Inequality: Income Inequality and Belief in Meritocracy Go Hand in Hand." *Socio-Economic Review* 19(1): 7–35.

Morphew, C. C., and M. Hartley. 2006. "Mission Statements: A Thematic Analysis of Rhetoric across Institutional Type." *The Journal of Higher Education* 77(3): 456–471.

Mucha, S. 2021. "Asian American Representation in Congress at Record High." *Axios*. Accessed October 17, 2021. https://www.axios.com/asian-american-congress-representation-7e573504-5b63-4627-8524-1947dd81e393.html

National Center for Education Statistics. 2019. "Bachelor's Degrees Conferred by Postsecondary Institutions, by Race/Ethnicity and Field of Study: 2016–17 and 2017–18." *Institute of Education Sciences*. Accessed October 15, 2021. https://nces.ed.gov/programs/digest/d19/tables/dt19_322.30.asp

Ng, J. C., S. S. Lee, and Y. K. Pak. 2007. "Chapter 4 Contesting the Model Minority and Perpetual Foreigner Stereotypes: A Critical Review of Literature on Asian Americans in Education." *Review of Research in Education* 31(1): 95–130.

Office for Fair Access. 2021. "Access Agreements: How We Regulate

Access Agreements Approved Under the Previous Regulatory System." *UK Office for Students*. Accessed October 24, 2021. https://www.officeforstudents.org.uk/advice-and-guidance /promoting-equal-opportunities/access-agreements/

Okechukwu, A. 2019. *To Fulfill These Rights: Political Struggle over Affirmative Action and Open Admissions*. New York: Columbia University Press.

Owens, A. 2020. "Unequal Opportunity: School and Neighborhood Segregation in the USA." *Race and Social Problems* 12(1): 29–41.

Pager, D., and H. Shepherd. 2008. "The Sociology of Discrimination: Racial Discrimination in Employment, Housing, Credit, and Consumer Markets." *Annual Review of Sociology* 34(1): 181–209.

Pew Research Center. 2017. "Chinese in the U.S. Fact Sheet." Accessed August 7, 2020. https://www.pewsocialtrends.org/fact -sheet/asian-americans-chinese-in-the-u-s/

Poon, O. A., M. S. Segoshi, L. Tang, K. L. Surla, C. Nguyen, and D. D. Squire. 2019. "Asian Americans, Affirmative Action, and the Political Economy of Racism: a Multidimensional Model of Raceclass Frames." *Harvard Educational Review* 89(2): 201–226.

President's Commission on Slavery and the University. n.d. "Universities Studying Slavery." *University of Virginia*. Accessed December 15, 2021. https://slavery.virginia.edu/universities -studying-slavery/

Rabinowitz, J. L., D. O. Sears, J. Sidanius, and J. A. Krosnick. 2009. "Why Do White Americans Oppose Race-Targeted Policies? Clarifying the Impact of Symbolic Racism." *Political Psychology* 30(5): 805–828.

Rachlinski, J. J., S. L. Johnson, A. J. Wistrich, and C. Guthrie. 2008. "Does Unconscious Racial Bias Affect Trial Judges." *Notre Dame Law Review* 84(3): 1195–1246.

References

Ray, R., and A. Gibbons. 2021. "Why Are States Banning Critical Race Theory?" *Brookings Institution*. Accessed April 1, 2022. https://www.brookings.edu/blog/fixgov/2021/07/02/why-are -states-banning-critical-race-theory/#_edn1

Reardon, S. F. 2016. "School Segregation and Racial Academic Achievement Gaps." *RSF: The Russell Sage Foundation Journal of the Social Sciences* 2(5): 34–57.

Redford, J., J. Ralph, and K. M. Hoyer. 2017. "First-Generation and Continuing-Generation College Students: A Comparison of High School and Postsecondary Experiences." *National Center for Education Statistics*. Accessed October 16, 2021. https://nces.ed. gov/pubs2018/2018009.pdf

Reyes, K. 2018. "Affirmative Action Shouldn't Be about Diversity." *The Atlantic*. Accessed April 1, 2022. https://www-theatlantic-com /ideas/archive/2018/12/affirmative-action-about-reparations-not -diversity/578005/

Rimer, S., and K. Arenson. 2004. "Top Colleges Take More Blacks, but Which Ones?" *The New York Times*. Accessed April 22, 2015. http://www.nytimes.com/2004/06/24/us/top-colleges-take-more -blacks-but-which-ones.html

Robinson, K., and A. L. Harris. 2014. *The Broken Compass: Parental Involvement with Children's Education*. Cambridge, MA: Harvard University Press.

Rothstein, R. 2017. *The Color of Law: A Forgotten History of How Our Government Segregated America*. New York: Liveright.

Saichaie, K., and C. C. Morphew. 2014. "What College and University Websites Reveal about the Purposes of Higher Education." *The Journal of Higher Education* 85(4): 499–530.

Salinas, C., and A. Lozano. 2021. "The history and evolution of the term Latinx." In *Handbook of Latinos and Education: Theory, Research, and Practice*, edited by Enrique G. Murillo Jr. et al. New York: Routledge.

References

Sandel, M. J. 1998. "Justice and the Good." In *Liberalism and the Limits of Justice*. Ed. M. J. Sandel. Cambridge, UK: Cambridge University Press.

Sandel, M. J. 2020. *The Tyranny of Merit: What's Become of the Common Good?* New York: Farrar, Straus and Giroux.

Sander, R. H. 2012. *Mismatch: How Affirmative Action Hurts Students It's Intended to Help, and Why Universities Won't Admit It*. New York: Basic Books.

Schwartz, B. 2005. "Top Colleges Should Select Randomly From a Pool Of 'Good Enough'." *Chronicle of Higher Education* 51(25): B20–B25.

Sears, D. O., and P. J. Henry. 2003. "The Origins of Symbolic Racism." *Journal of Personality & Social Psychology* 85(2): 259–275.

Seltzer, R. 2020. "How Much Are Most Colleges Paying in Endowment Tax?" *Inside Higher Ed.* Accessed October 24, 2021. https://www.insidehighered.com/news/2020/02/18/wealthiest-universities-are-paying-big-endowment-tax-bills-how-much-are-others-who

Sen, A. 2000. "Merit and Justice." In *Meritocracy and Economic Inequality*. Ed. K. Arrow, S. Bowles, and S. Durlauf. Princeton, NJ: Princeton University Press.

Sharkey, P. 2013. *Stuck in Place: Urban Neighborhoods and the End of Progress toward Racial Equality*. Chicago, IL: The University of Chicago Press.

Shedd, C. 2015. *Unequal City: Race, Schools, and Perceptions of Injustice*. New York: Russell Sage Foundation.

Shelby County v. Holder. 2003. 570 U.S. 529.

Sidanius, J., S. Levin, C. van Laar, and D. O. Sears. 2008. *The Diversity Challenge: Social Identity and Intergroup Relations on the College Campus*. New York: Russell Sage Foundation.

Skiba, R. J., R. H. Horner, C.-G. Chung, M. K. Rausch, S. L. May, and T. Tobin. 2011. "Race Is Not Neutral: A National Investigation of African American and Latino Disproportionality in School Discipline." *School Psychology Review* 40(1): 85–107.

Smith, C. 2017. "Affirmative Action as Reparations." *The New Republic.* Accessed April 1, 2022. https://newrepublic.com/article/144676/affirmative-action-reparations

Snellman, K., J. M. Silva, C. B. Frederick, and R. D. Putnam. 2015. "The Engagement Gap: Social Mobility and Extracurricular Participation among American Youth." *The ANNALS of the American Academy of Political and Social Science* 657(1): 194–207.

Soares, J. 2011. *SAT Wars: The Case for Test-Optional College Admissions.* New York: Teachers College Press.

Starck, J. G., T. Riddle, S. Sinclair, and N. Warikoo. 2020. "Teachers Are People Too: Examining the Racial Bias of Teachers Compared to Other American Adults." *Educational Researcher* 49(4): 273–284.

Steele, C. M., and J. Aronson. 1995. "Stereotype Threat and the Intellectual Test Performance of African Americans." *Journal of Personality & Social Psychology* 69(5): 797–811.

Stevens, M. 2007. *Creating a Class: College Admissions and the Education of Elites.* Cambridge: Harvard University Press.

Stone, P. 2013. "Access to Higher Education by the Luck of the Draw." *Comparative Education Review* 57(3): 577–599.

Students for Fair Admissions, Inc. v. President and Fellows of Harvard College. 2019. 397 F. Supp. 3d 126 (D. Mass.).

Stulberg, L. M., and A. S. Chen. 2014. "The Origins of Race-conscious Affirmative Action in Undergraduate Admissions: A Comparative Analysis of Institutional Change in Higher Education." *Sociology of Education* 87(1): 36–52.

Swarns, R. 2008. "Delicate Obama Path on Class and Race Preferences." *The New York Times.* Accessed October 17, 2021. https://www.nytimes.com/2008/08/03/us/politics/03affirmative.html

Swarns, R. 2016. "Georgetown University Plans Steps to Atone for Slave Past." *The New York Times.* Accessed October 17, 2021. https://www.nytimes.com/2016/09/02/us/slaves-georgetown

References

-university.html?emc=edit_na_20160901&nlid=68893759&ref =cta

Swarns, R. 2019. "Is Georgetown's $400,000-a-Year Plan to Aid Slave Descendants Enough?" *The New York Times*. Accessed October 17, 2021. https://www.nytimes.com/2019/10/30/us/georgetown -slavery-reparations.html

Tran, V. C., J. Lee, and T. J. Huang. 2019. "Revisiting the Asian Second-Generation Advantage." *Ethnic and Racial Studies* 42(13): 2248–2269.

Walia, H. 2021. *Border and Rule: Global Migration, Capitalism, and the Rise of Racist Nationalism*. Chicago, IL: Haymarket Books.

Warikoo, N. 2016. *The Diversity Bargain: And Other Dilemmas of Race, Admissions, and Meritocracy at Elite Universities*. Chicago, IL: University of Chicago Press.

Warikoo, N. 2019. "Why Elite Colleges Should Use a Lottery to Admit Students." *The Conversation*. Accessed April 8, 2019. https:// theconversation.com/why-elite-colleges-should-use-a-lottery-to -admit-students-108799

Warikoo, N. 2022. *Race at the Top: Asian Americans and Whites in Pursuit of the American Dream in Suburban Schools*. Chicago, IL: University of Chicago Press.

Warikoo, N., and U. Allen. 2020. "A Solution to Multiple Problems: The Origins of Affirmative Action in Higher Education Around the World." *Studies in Higher Education* 45(12): 2398–2412.

Weissbourd, R., J. Weissbourd, J. Murray, T. R. Anderson, T. Nicola, and B. Barnard. 2021. "Innovation and Justice: Reinventing Selective Colleges." *Making Caring Common*. Accessed October 17, 2021. https://static1.squarespace.com/static /5b7c56e255b02c683659fe43/t/607985ebd85c490108b1d83c /1618576875736/Reinventing+Selective+Colleges+2021_04_14. pdf

References

Westrick, P. A., J. P. Marini, L. Young, H. Ng, D. Shmueli, and E. J. Shaw. 2019. "Validity of the SAT for Predicting First-Year Grades and Retention to the Second Year." *College Board.* Accessed October 18, 2021. https://www.researchgate.net/profile/Paul-Westrick /publication/334262776_Validity_of_the_SATR_for_Predicting _First-Year_Grades_and_Retention_to_the_Second_Year/links /5d1f8363299bf1547c9b8660/Validity-of-the-SATR-for-Predicting-First-Year-Grades-and-Retention-to-the-Second-Year.pdf

Williams, H. A. 2012. *Help Me to Find My People: The African American Search for Family Lost in Slavery.* Chapel Hill: The University of North Carolina Press.

Wu, E. D. 2014. *The Color of Success: Asian Americans and the Origins of the Model Minority.* Princeton, NJ: Princeton University Press.

Yi, V. and S. D. Museus. 2015. "Model Minority Myth." In *Wiley Blackwell Encyclopedia of Race, Ethnicity, and Nationalism.* Ed. A. D. Smith, X. Hou, J. Stone, R. Dennis and P. Rizova. Hoboken, NJ: Wiley.

Zuberi, T., and E. Bonilla-Silva. 2008. *White Logic, White Methods: Racism and Methodology.* Lanham, MD: Rowman & Littlefield Publishers.

Zwick, R. 2017. *Who Gets In? Strategies for Fair and Effective College Admissions.* Cambridge, MA: Harvard University Press.

Introduction

1 Affirmative action is only relevant when there are more applicants than spots. Hence, it is not relevant at open-access
colleges and those that have similar numbers of applicants and
seats.

2 Carney 1995.

3 Gallup 2018.

4 Carey, Clayton, and Horiuchi 2019.

5 Davern et al., 1972–2021.

6 Kehal, Hirschman, and Berrey 2021.

7 Counsel for President and Fellows of Harvard College, 2018.

8 In this book I use "Black" and "African American" inter-
changeably. I use the gender neutral "Latinx" to indicate anyone
with ancestry in Latin America (similar to "Hispanic" on the
US Census). See Salinas and Lozano 2021 for a discussion of
"Latinx." Despite diverse racial identities in official reporting,
Latinx are considered eligible for affirmative action given that
they are generally seen as racial minorities.

9 *Harvard Gazette*, "Unprecedented Admissions Year" 2011;
Gartsbeyn 2021; Lu and Tsotsong 2021.

10 Duru-Bellat and Tenret 2012; Lipset 1975.

11 Bellah 1985.

12 Okechukwu 2019.

13 Berrey 2015; Okechukwu 2019.

14 Ballotpedia n.d.; Okechukwu 2019.
15 Berrey 2015; Okechukwu 2019.
16 Bobo 1998; Rabinowitz, Sears, Sidanius, and Krosnick 2009.
17 Bonilla-Silva 2003; Warikoo 2016.
18 Epps 2014.
19 Bobo and Kluegel 1993; Sears and Henry 2003.
20 For example, see Sander 2012.
21 On wealth differences, see Johnson 2006. On neighborhoods, see Iceland and Wilkes 2014. On perceptions of Americanness, see Cheryan and Monin 2005. On perceptions of warmth, see Lin, Kwan, Cheung, and Fiske 2005.
22 Dworkin 1977; Dworkin 2012; Sandel 1998; Sen 2000.
23 Dworkin 1977; Dworkin 2012; Sandel 1998; Sen 2000.
24 Karabel 2005.
25 Fishman 2020; Hsin and Xie 2014.
26 Batalova, Hanna, and Levesque 2021.

Chapter 1: The Purposes of Higher Education and the History of Affirmative Action

1 National Center for Education Statistics 2019.
2 Hextrum 2018; Jayakumar and Page 2021.
3 Kerr 2001.
4 Kerr 2001.
5 Morphew and Hartley 2006.
6 Morphew and Hartley 2006.
7 Kohli 2015.
8 Saichaie and Morphew 2014.
9 The US News and World Report rankings played a significant role in colleges' efforts to improve their average test scores. Espeland and Sauder 2007.
10 Guinier 2015.

11 Stevens 2007.
12 Sandel 1998, 142.
13 Anderson 2021; Diaz 2020.
14 Johnson 1965.
15 Stulberg and Chen 2014.
16 Okechukwu 2019.
17 Unlike the United States, some countries mandate affirmative action in their constitutions, shielding it from legal contestation. Warikoo and Allen 2020.
18 Berrey 2015; Okechukwu 2019.
19 *Fisher v. Texas* 2013; *Fisher v. Texas* 2016; *Gratz v. Bollinger* 2003; *Grutter v. Bollinger* 2003.
20 Liptak and Hartocollis 2022.
21 Blum's goal of ending all race-based protections of underrepresented minorities goes back to his role in the Supreme Court's *Shelby County v. Holder* decision, which ended voting rights protections designed to ensure the right to vote for racial minorities. *Shelby v. Holder* 2003. It is important to note, too, that in the affirmative action cases Blum has not addressed the anti-Asian discrimination he suggests exists in admissions by asking for anti-Asian bias training for admissions officers; nor has he sought the end of other policies that privilege whites over Asian Americans, such as legacy admissions. Rather, he seems to be using Asian Americans exclusively to further his goal of the end of the consideration of race in admission for underrepresented minorities.

Chapter 2: The Case For and Against Affirmative Action

1 Hutchings and Valentino 2004.
2 Antonio 2001; Bowman 2010; Chang 1999; Fischer 2008; Gurin 1999; Gurin, Dey, Hurtado, and Gurin 2002.

3 Laar, Levin, Sinclair, and Sidanius 2005.
4 Bowen and Bok 1998; Bowman 2011; Chang 1999; Gurin 1999; Jayakumar 2008; Sidanius, Levin, van Laar, and Sears 2008.
5 Hoxby and Avery 2012.
6 Barnes 2014; Swarns 2008.
7 Dee 2004.
8 Huerto and Lindo 2020.
9 Rachlinski, Johnson, Wistrich, and Guthrie 2008.
10 Bowen and Bok 1998.
11 Bleemer 2021.
12 Mijs 2021. Across countries, Mijs also finds that the more unequal a society the more likely people in that country believe that those unequal social positions are deserved and earned through meritocratic processes.
13 Stulberg and Chen 2014.
14 As cited in Warikoo 2016.
15 Katznelson 2005.
16 Katznelson 2005.
17 Massey and Denton 1993; Rothstein 2017.
18 Choi, Herbert, and Winslow 2019; Lacy 2007; Pager and Shepherd 2008.
19 Johnson 2006; Massey and Denton 1993.
20 Johnson 2006.
21 McIntosh, Moss, Nunn, and Shambaugh 2020.
22 Owens 2020.
23 Alba, Logan, and Stults 2000; Sharkey 2013.
24 Reardon 2016.
25 Owens 2020.
26 Harris 2021.
27 Harris 2021.
28 Starck, Riddle, Sinclair, and Warikoo 2020.

29 Chin, Quinn, Dhaliwal, and Lovison 2020; Jacoby-Senghor, Sinclair, and Shelton 2016.

30 Lewis and Diamond 2015; Shedd 2015; Skiba, Horner, Chung, Rausch, May, and Tobin 2011.

31 Redford, Ralph, and Hoyer 2017.

32 Carnevale and Strohl 2013.

33 Westrick, Marini, Young, Ng, Shmueli, and Shaw 2019.

34 Kaushal, Magnuson, and Waldfogel 2011; Snellman, Silva, Frederick, and Putnam 2015.

35 Bowen and Levin 2003; Hextrum 2018; Jayakumar and Page 2021.

36 Berrey 2011; Okechukwu 2019; Warikoo 2016.

37 Reyes 2018; Smith 2017.

38 For example, see Coates 2014; Darity 2020.

39 Bosman 2021.

40 Fandos 2021.

41 Walia 2021.

42 Brown University Steering Committee on Slavery and Justice n.d.

43 For example, see President's Commission on Slavery and the University n.d.

44 Swarns 2016.

45 Swarns 2019.

46 This justification requires discussion of whether Black immigrants should benefit, given that their ancestors were not harmed by slavery on US soil. Indeed, some scholars have questioned whether the children of Black immigrants should be the beneficiaries of affirmative action, especially when they seem to substitute for African American students who were the first intended beneficiaries. Massey, Mooney, Charles, and Torres 2007; Rimer and Arenson 2004.

47 Warikoo 2016.

48 Ray and Gibbons 2021; *Shelby v. Holder* 2003.

49 Okechukwu 2019.

50 Bonilla-Silva 2003; Hagerman 2018; Lewis-McCoy 2014; Warikoo 2016.

51 On class instead of race, see Kahlenberg 1996. On the use of zip code over race, see Cashin 2015.

52 Hutchings and Valentino 2004.

53 Harris 2011; Robinson and Harris 2014.

54 Dow 2019; Lareau 2011.

55 Warikoo 2022.

56 Williams 2012.

57 Swarns 2019. McMillan Cottom argues that Georgetown's policy is not, in fact, a form of reparations, because it does not provide financial compensation for gains from slavery. McMillan Cottom 2016.

58 Bobo and Kluegel 1993.

59 Sander 2012. See also Arcidiacono, Aucejo, and Hotz 2016.

60 For a summary of studies that critically analyze mismatch theory, see Kidder 2013; Bleemer 2020.

61 See also Dale and Krueger 2002; Dale and Krueger 2011.

62 Alon and Tienda 2005; Carnevale and Strohl 2013.

63 Bleemer 2021.

64 Bleemer 2021.

65 Arcidiacono, Aucejo, and Hotz 2016; Sander 2012.

66 See Bleemer 2020; Kidder 2013 for detailed analyses of data on mismatch theory.

67 Bell 1979.

Chapter 3: Asian Americans, Achievement, and Affirmative Action

1 For example, see *Students for Fair Admissions v. President and Fellows of Harvard College* 2019.

2 Hsu 2018; Poon, et al. 2019.

3 Kochhar and Cilluffo 2018.

4 Chin 2020; Huang 2021; Laforce 2018; Mucha 2021.

5 Chin 2020; Tran, Lee, and Huang 2019.

6 Yi and Museus 2015.

7 Li and Wang 2008; Ng, Lee, and Pak 2007. For a history of the model minority idea, see Wu 2014.

8 Krogstad and Radford 2018.

9 Of course, not all Asian immigrants arrive through the route of highly skilled migration. Overall, Asian Americans are the most bifurcated group in the US socioeconomically: the gap between high-income Asian Americans and low-income Asian Americans is greater than the gap for all other race groups in the United States. Kochhar and Cilluffo 2018. Even among Chinese Americans, the largest Asian group in the US, 13 percent live in poverty. Pew Research Center 2017. Additionally, 1.7 million Asians in the US are unauthorized; that number is rapidly growing. Esterline and Batalova 2022.

10 Krogstad and Radford 2018.

11 See Lee and Zhou 2015; Warikoo 2022.

12 Carson 2003; Zuberi and Bonilla-Silva 2008.

13 Geismer 2015; Massey and Denton 1993.

14 Alba 2020.

15 Levin 2021.

16 Cheryan and Monin 2005; Fiske, Xu, Cuddy, and Glick 1999; Kim 1999; Lin, Kwan, Cheung, and Fiske 2005.

17 Lee and Zhou 2015.

18 Fiske, Xu, Cuddy, and Glick 1999.

19 Steele and Aronson 1995.

20 McKown and Weinstein 2008.

21 Chin 2020; Kim 1999; Tran, Lee, and Huang 2019.

22 Kim 1999.

23 *Students for Fair Admissions v. President and Fellows of Harvard College* 2019.

Conclusion: From Fairness to Justice

1 Bleemer 2021; Long and Bateman 2020.
2 On colleges comparing upward, see Espeland and Sauder 2016. Still, recent studies show that less selective colleges are moving away from affirmative action, and those that say they practice affirmative action have also seen drops in minority enrollment, even as Harvard has affirmed its commitment to affirmative action by holding steadfast amidst the *SFFA vs. Harvard* trial. Hirschman and Berrey 2017; Kehal, Hirschman, and Berrey 2021.
3 Blair and Smetters 2021.
4 See for example, Westrick, Marini, Young, Ng, Shmueli, and Shaw 2019.
5 Soares 2011.
6 Bennett 2022.
7 Alvero, Giebel, Gebre-Medhin, Lising Antonio, Stevens, and Domingue 2021.
8 Belasco, Rosinger, and Hearn 2015. More recent studies, which include a broader range of colleges beyond liberal arts colleges, do find a small increase in underrepresented minorities and economically disadvantaged students when colleges, especially larger and less selective colleges, go test-optional. Bennett 2022.
9 Blair and Smetters 2021; Kirp 2021; Weissbourd, Weissbourd, Murray, Anderson, Nicola, and Barnard 2021.
10 Graham 2014.
11 Blair and Smetters 2021; Brint and Karabel 1989.
12 Blair and Smetters 2021.
13 Office for Fair Access 2021.

14 Hartocollis 2019.
15 Daugherty, McFarlin, and Martorell 2014; Long, Saenz, and Tienda 2010.
16 Black, Denning, and Rothstein 2020.
17 Cortes 2010; Cortes and Klasik 2021; Long and Tienda 2008.
18 Cullen, Long, and Reback 2013.
19 Carnevale and Strohl 2013; Espinosa, Turk, Taylor, and Chessman 2019.
20 Harris 2021.
21 Ma, Pender, and Libassi 2020.
22 Avery, Hoxby, Jackson, Burek, Pope, and Raman 2006; C. J. Dynarski, Libassi, Michelmore, and Owen 2020.
23 McMillan Cottom 2017.
24 Brint 2019.
25 Hamilton and Nielsen 2021.
26 Seltzer 2020.
27 Seltzer 2020.
28 To see which colleges are most effective at promoting social mobility, see Aisch et al. 2017.
29 Office for Fair Access 2021.
30 Alon and Tienda 2007.
31 Others have also suggested some form of an admissions lottery, including Guinier 2001; Sandel 2020; Schwartz 2005; Stone 2013; Warikoo 2019. For critiques of admissions lotteries, see Baker and Bastedo 2022; Grofman and Merrill 2004; Zwick 2017. Some critics have pointed out that SAT- and GPA-based lotteries can reduce the number of underrepresented minority students admitted; this is because that method does not use holistic review.
32 For example, see the histories of University of Illinois and Dutch medical school admissions, as cited in Zwick 2017, 163–164.

Index

Index

Index